Through the Northern Looking Glass

Through the Northern Looking Glass

Breast Cancer Stories Told by Northern Native Women

LORELEI ANNE LAMBERT COLOMEDA, PhD, RN

NLN Press • New York

Pub. No. 14-6827

Quotes from *Athabascan Legend* are used with permission from Epicenter Press, Seattle, Washington.
Cover photo: Inukshuck, Baffin Island Arctic Canada by Frank Tyro— Used with permission. .

The views expressed in this book reflect those of the authors and do not necessarily reflect the official views of the National League for Nursing.

Library of Congress Cataloging-in-Publication Data

Lambert Colomeda, Lorelei Anne.
  Through the Northern looking glass : breast cancer stories told by Northern native women / Lorelei Anne Lambert Colomeda.
      p.   cm.
  Includes bibliographical references and index.
  "Pub. no. 6827."
  ISBN 0-88737-682-7
  1. Breast—Cancer—Canada, Northern. 2. Breast—Cancer—Alaska.
3. Indian women—Diseases—Canada, Northern. 4. Indian women— Diseases—Alaska. 5. Medical geography. 6. Medical anthropology.
I. Title.
RC280.B8L273   1996
306.4'61—dc20   96-18865
                                                                         CIP

This book was set in Bodoni by Publications Development Company, Crockett, Texas. The editor and designer was Allan Graubard. The printer was Bookcrafters. The cover was designed by Lauren Stevens.

Printed in the United States of America.

This work is dedicated to Pat and Joann. Your courageous journeys with breast cancer and with death gave me inspiration and hope. You are never forgotten and forever loved.

Royalties from this work will be placed in scholarship at Salish Kootenai College, Pablo, Montana, in support of Native American Breast Cancer research.

ABOUT THE AUTHOR

*L*orelei (Lori) Lambert Colomeda, PhD, RN, is a medical ecologist who spent her early youth in Boston, Massachusetts, where she graduated from nursing school. Dr. Colomeda is the Kellogg Grant Coordinator at Salish Kootenai College, Pablo, Montana, where she teaches courses in ecological health, environmental health, environmental ethics, and is the distance education liaison for the nursing department.

Before Salish Kootenai College, Dr. Colomeda worked in the Philippines and for 12 years was the education director in environmental science at the Schuylkill Center in Philadelphia, a satellite campus for Beaver College. She has presented at a number of conferences, including the Canadian Bioethics Society Conference in Vancouver, British Columbia, and the Rural Nursing Conference in Bozeman, Montana. She lives in Pablo, Montana, with her husband, Frank Tyro, two dogs, Rosie Bear and Katiya Wolf, and a cat named Kit.

CONTENTS

FOREWORD

*T*he health of contemporary Arctic peoples is a paradox. Children's health in the widely dispersed, isolated settlements of Alaska and northern Canada has improved considerably in the last forty years. At mid-century, tuberculosis, polio, ear infections, and measles were epidemic. In the 1960s, there were 124 deaths per 1,000 Inuit infants in the larger eastern Arctic settlements, comparable to rates in the poorest of Third World nations (Hobart, 1975). Today the infant mortality rate among Inuit has fallen to 19 per 1,000 (Muir, 1991), still high but much improved over the past. Through primary health care programs, the average life expectancy for Inuit in Canada has risen to 66 years.

On the other hand, as Lori Colomeda's remarkable study shows, the incidence of "modern" diseases is rising sharply among adults in the North. Cancer is the second leading cause of death among Northern Native people, accounting for 18 percent of Inuit deaths and 12 percent in Indians in 1990. Among native men, lung cancer is the most prevalent form of cancer. In women, cervical cancer is highest and lung cancer second highest. Increasing numbers of women are being diagnosed as having breast cancer as well. Thus the paradox: medicine and public health have reduced infectious disease but cannot prevent the so-called "diseases of civilization," the degenerative, often environmentally-caused diseases that affect industrialized societies. Children enjoy good health, but adults face new risks.

The etiology of cancer in the North is complex. It is surely related to toxic waste and contamination of water and the food chain with potentially carcinogenic chemicals. Organochlorines (PCBs or polychlorinated biphenyls) have been detected in Broughton Island, in northeastern Canada, in the meat of seals, walrus, and caribou, and in narwhal skin. These animals are all important sources of food for the Inuit, and the toxicants from their flesh accumulate gradually in human tissue. Testing of human tissue samples showed that 63 percent of the children had PCB levels above acceptable contamination levels (Kinloch & Kuhnlein, 1988). Almost half of the men aged forty-five to sixty-five showed higher than acceptable levels of contaminant intake (Muir, 1991). Colomeda's study documents similar chemical exposure in Arctic Quebec, as well as nuclear waste contamination near Point Hope, Alaska.

Cancer incidence is also related to the heavy use of chewing and smoking tobacco. Smoking is part of the northern frontier culture. The practice begins early: between the ages of ten and fourteen, 16 percent of Inuit girls and 13 percent of Inuit boys in the Northwest Territories are regular smokers. By the age of nineteen, 45 percent of native males and 52 percent of females are regular smokers. For many, smoking becomes a lifelong addiction, and few women stop even during pregnancy. Similar patterns of tobacco use are found in Alaska.

A third factor is lack of diagnostic care and early screening for cancer, partly due to the difficult logistics and costs of transporting mammographic equipment to isolated settlements. Northern communities in Alaska and Canada are terribly underserved. *Through the Northern Looking Glass* takes us to a strange land, indeed, where women have little preventive care or training in self-examination. It is a place where toxic waste leaches into rivers and oceans; where radiation diffuses from Chernobyl and other sites of contamination, entering the food chain through the lichens that caribou eat. It is a land where women who have traditionally breastfed their children for two or three years are now afraid to because traces of organochlorines have been found in their milk. With no access to the simple and inexpensive Pap test that has been available to most North Americans for decades, cervical cancer is the leading cause of death from cancer for Northern Native Women. These shocking facts underscore the point that health is a function of politics as well as of ecology. In the North, women have the double disadvantage of gender discrimination and ethnic marginalization in health care.

Balancing critical inquiry and compassion in its portrayal of women's experiences with breast cancer, Colomeda's study represents medical ecology at its best. This work systematically demonstrates interactions among environment, culture, and health. I know of no other source that so effectively describes environmental and economic impacts and constraints on native women's health.

Skillfully blending several methodologies and perspectives, Colomeda integrates reflexive analysis of her role as ethnographer and her personal history with the subjects' illness narratives and life histories. The history of the North, legends, and symbolism are interwoven into the analysis, giving us rich ethnographic context. Colomeda accomplishes what an epidemiologist or clinician could not, constructing an ethno-ecological profile of breast cancer in all its clinical, behavioral, and cultural complexity. The work is grounded in individual narratives of incredible bravery and resilience against the backdrop of profound cultural and environmental transformations.

It is not possible to remain detached while reading this book. Colomeda writes with an intensity born of her own family's history. There is much to learn from this work, not only in an anthropological or clinical sense, but in a personal sense as well. All of us know someone who has lived with this disease, and many of us will face our own diagnosis of some form of cancer, given the ubiquitous carcinogens in our environments and the multiple insults to our immune systems. As I read, memories surfaced of my paternal grandmother who died from cervical cancer when I was six years old. I was also reminded of friends who have more recently encountered cancer, some surviving and others not. Through this book, I have increased my understanding of the impact of cancer on women's lives and I have a greater awareness of the importance of social networks in coping with and adapting to the disease.

Remarkably, the voices in these interviews are resigned, resolute, stoic—not angry. It is clear that Lori Colomeda approached them with deep respect, allowing them to speak as survivors, not as victims. Most of the women do not perceive their poor health as a political issue; nor do they blame themselves. There is pain, but little self-pity, and there are honest accounts of journeys through depression, isolation, substance abuse, and eventual self-healing.

Often, relationships are strengthened rather than weakened by the woman's illness. Colomeda writes, "it was heartening to discover the emotional support, the love and partnership, that Northern Native men gave to their women. . . . They stood by through chemotherapy, vomiting, hair loss, depression, and continued to love their wives and care for them." Colomeda sees the disease experience as having *empowered* the women she interviewed, giving them purpose to live as well as possible and to fight against despair and hopelessness.

In medical ecology, which influenced Colomeda's work, health and environment are linked in an equilibrium model, which holds that a population with the resources to respond adequately to the challenges and constraints of the environment has a high potential for health.

This model works well in bounded habitats, but it is more difficult to use when intrusive elements enter the region. In contemporary northern communities, the equation of ecological balance and health is modified by a third critical element, political economy. Access to resources, the ability to procure food, housing, and health care, exposure to hazards, and ultimately health patterns are as much influenced by national and global economic forces as by local ecology (McElroy, 1996). Colomeda's study gives testimony to the fact that integration of ecological and political approaches is not only possible but is also highly productive, representing the best of a new generation of medical anthropology research. Lori Colomeda is to be commended for bringing her energy and clarity of vision to this task.

Ann McElroy, PhD
Department of Anthropology
State University of New York at Buffalo

REFERENCES

Hobart, C. W. (1975). Socioeconomic correlates of mortality and morbidity among Inuit infants. *Arctic Anthropology 12*, 37–48.

Kaufert, P. A. (1996). Women and the debate over mammography: An economic, political, and moral history. In C. F. Sargent & C. B. Brettell (Eds.), *Gender and Health: An International Perspective* (pp. 167–186). Upper Saddle River, NJ: Prentice-Hall.

Kinloch, D., & Kuhnlein, H. (1988). Assessment of PCBs in arctic foods and diets—A pilot study in Broughton Island, Northwest Territories, Canada. *Circumpolar Health, 87*, 159–162.

McElroy, A. (1996). Modernization, social change, and health in the eastern Arctic. In M. Foller & L. Hansson (Eds.), *Human ecology and health: Adaptation to a changing world* (pp. 72–93). Goteborg University.

Muir, B. L. (1991). *Health status of Canadian Indians and Inuit—1990.* Indian and Northern Health Services, Medical Services Branch, Health and Welfare Canada.

Sherwin, S. (1996). Cancer and women: Some feminist ethics concerns. In C. F. Sargent & C. B. Brettell (Eds.), *Gender and health: An international perspective* (pp. 187–204). Upper Saddle River, NJ: Prentice-Hall.

ACKNOWLEDGMENTS

*T*his project would not have been possible without help from many others. I am grateful to the following who gave me inspiration, courage, guidance, and assistance: My grandmothers Domithilde Gogeun, Leda Roi Arsenault, Ann McKenna; my grandfathers Eustache Lambert, Calixte Arsenault, George Dewey Arsenault, who died of metastatic lung cancer; my father Joseph Henri Lambert, who died of metastatic prostate cancer; my grandmother Ann Arsenault and my mother Marie Arsenault Lambert Kadehjian, who showed me how to be brave through their breast cancer; my stepfather Edward Kadehjian for his love and devotion and for his bravery in facing prostate cancer. They have taught me respect, honor, and how to survive. I also thank my brother Laurent Peter Lambert for researching our family history. His curiosity gave impetus to my work. I would also like to thank my children Regina, Emily, and Ted for their patience and love.

The following individuals have given me guidance, and support: Dr. Marlene Ryan Warner of the Union Institute, for her friendship, her laughter, and her late night phone calls; Dr. Sanford Searl of the Union Institute, whose feedback helped to focus my work; Dr. Janet Mancini Billson of George Washington University, who blazed the trail to the Arctic; Dr. James Halfpenny, former Director of the Mountain Research Station of the University of Colorado, for his friendship, guidance, and for a wonderful internship in Alaska; Dr. Greg Bachman, chair of the Film Studies

Department, University of Tampa, for his friendship, e-mails, and words of encouragement; Dr. Valerie Dively of Galludet University, who taught me about deaf culture; Whitney Carpenter, Montgomery County Community College, who taught me to focus my expository writing—he always knew I would do it; and Nancy Christie of the Schuylkill Center for Environmental Education in Philadelphia for her friendship and inspiration in environmental education.

I must also thank Dr. Norman London of the Canadian Embassy, Washington, DC, whose office of Academic Affairs partially funded my original study through a doctoral fellowship research grant. Thank you also to the following medical officers who helped me in Canada and Alaska: Dr. Robert Bowerman, Chief Medical Officer Borough of Barrow; Dr. Ian Gilchrist, Yellowknife; Dr. Bruce Johnson, Baffin Regional Hospital, Iqaluit, N.W.T., Canada; Judy Applin-Poole RN, Curtis Memorial Hospital Grenfell Mission, St. Anthony's Newfoundland for her untiring efforts in smoothing the way so that my work could take place in Labrador, December 1993; thank you also to Claudette Amadon, RN, OCN, outpatient oncology coordinator at Alaska Native Medical Center, Anchorage. Claudette spent many hours coordinating patient interviews in Alaska. Without her help, I would not have been able to do research in Anchorage in the summer of 1994. My sincere thanks to Allan Graubard, director of NLN Press, for his editorial leadership: "Pooyai!" I thank all of the women who participated in the project; all of the families who accepted me into their homes. Without their eagerness and openness, there would be no project. I must also thank my father-in-law and mother-in-law, Hilbert and Marion Seines, who gave me access to their ranch in Round Butte, Montana, and provided a place to write in their beautiful red barn, overlooking the inspirational Mission Mountains. Thank you also to Frank Tyro [Ty Wolf] for support, advice, many hours of reading drafts, many hours of taping interviews, and for loving companionship in the glorious North!

LALC

INTRODUCTION

*T*he far North is a vast expanse of rugged, rocky, and often mountainous land that scientists define in a variety of ways: North begins at the Arctic Circle or 66 degrees north latitude; North begins where the tree line ends; North begins at the edge of the permafrost, that dark layer of frozen soil found under the topsoil. For the purpose of this study, North is defined as any land mass north of 56 degrees north latitude. I chose this definition because of the latitude of Churchill, Manitoba, the place where I fell in love with North.

Globally, a variety of northern ecosystems are found from Siberia and Alaska to Canada and Svalbard, Sweden. They embrace habitats such as tundra, muskeg, and boreal forest. For those of us living in the temperate zone, we imagine North as wasteland locked under ice and snow. In some respects, this image is accurate since snow and ice, present in the latitudes of the high arctic, never melt in the summer. However, Northern ecosystems are also considered polar deserts, receiving very little moisture throughout the year. Because of the harsh cold, lack of moisture, and six months of darkness in winter, plants and animals have developed unique survival adaptations. For example, hairy plant stems conserve heat and water; plants grow in cushions and low to the ground to conserve heat; fiberoptic-like adaptations of mammal hair directs heat from the sun onto the black skin of harp seals and polar bears. Such harsh conditions maintain a sparsely human-populated ecosystem. In the mid-Arctic and in the latitudes lower than 56 degrees, the summer growing season with increased amounts of sunlight brings a profusion of

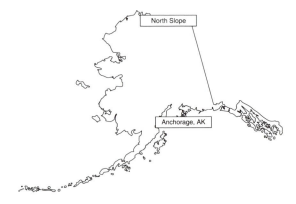

flowers, insects, birds, and mammals. It is in these mid-Arctic latitudes that larger populations of humans are able to survive.

A powerful force, as intense as the migration of caribou and tundra swans, draws me to this land as it drew my ancient ancestors. Much like an inner knowing, it is a force that cannot be explained. The work that leads me North propels me closer to Northern Native Women who survive in spite of the harshness of their lives in the boreal forest and tundra. It is these women who have delivered and cared for their newborn infants far from cities, clinics, hospitals, malls, and pharmacies; these women who have sewn clothing from caribou and seal to protect their men—hunters and providers—enabling them to survive. Like the land itself, it is the women who are its strength. Throughout history, women have also healed one another. In this book, I give voice to thirteen Northern Native Women who have traveled on an extraordinary journey with an assassin called breast cancer.

Among Native Peoples and especially Northern Native Women, the telling of stories and oral history has been a timeless, traditional path in which information is given and received. Oral history represents a woman's culture. It preserves her traditions, values, and way of life. The woman is the interpreter of her own lived experiences. The woman is the Keeper of the Wisdom, the Knower. Yet the breast cancer stories told here reflect other images and feelings: of lost womaness, of fear, of loneliness, of cultural isolation, of despair, and of mortality.

Thirteen women, thirteen voices—a chorus by which we gain a "lived experience" and find ways to answer to the following six questions: (1) What is the experience of Northern Native Women who have survived breast cancer? (2) What are their lives like? (3) How have they adapted and survived? (4) What message do they send to other women? (5) How do

Northern Native Women see themselves as their health is compromised by an increase in environmental contamination? (6) What are the commonalities among Native Women who live in northern environments and non-Native Women who do not?

While appearing pollution free, in reality the North acts as a great sink into which pollutants, arriving on air currents of the winds and oceans from the southern latitudes, are deposited. Pesticides and nuclear contamination have become problematic over the years. Although as yet there is no measurable link to the pollutants in the ecosystem, the rising incidence of breast cancer among the women who live there needs further investigation by medical ecologists.

The present work is biographical as well as topical and begins in Chapter 1 with my ancestral connection to the land, to Canada, and to breast cancer. Although I have spent much of my adult life in New England and Pennsylvania, my heritage spreads far into the Canadian North. The blood of Native People flowed through the bodies of my grandmothers and grandfathers. It flows through mine. My love for Canada, for Alaska, and for my native heritage has never been far from my vision—a vision of a wild, rugged, untamed land rich with uniquely adapted plants and animals. It is my hope, as well, to give voice to these now quiet ancestors—to honor them and the living Native Women in Canada and Alaska. The work satisfies my desperate longing to know how other women have survived breast cancer. In searching for their voices, I find my grandmothers. I find myself.

In Chapter 2, which outlines the images that women have of themselves as women, I also focus on historical views of Native Women from the perspective of native culture and male Eurocentric culture. In Chapter 3, I review the literature of breast cancer in which White Eurocentric women relate their experiences with breast cancer and describe changes in their personal image as a result. A section on methodology can be found in Appendix C. In Chapter 4, I present the voices of Native Women in northern environments who have had breast cancer. The women speak about changes in their lives as a result of the experience. They disclose how their family, culture, and education helped in healing. They encountered strength and healing in the telling of their stories. Some of the women live alone, others live with husbands, children, and grandchildren. Some live in cities; others live in remote villages. Finally, in Chapter 5, I conclude discussion on the six main questions with this finding: women who have survived breast cancer feel empowered.

Introduction

In researching the personal, biological, and cultural components of breast cancer issues with Northern Native Women, I also examine, through the paradigm of medical ecology, the clashing and blending of technological cultures with cultures of indigenous peoples. Medical ecology is a relatively new field of study developed under the spectrum of medical anthropology. To gain a clearer understanding of disease, medical ecologists examine aspects of anthropology and environmental health/contamination, with clinical and epidemiological data. Medical ecologists are interested in how the technology of the dominant culture impacts on the environment as well as the health of the nondominant or indigenous culture. As a medical ecologist, I feel that this work has a broad view and is important to other fields of study, especially nursing and the health sciences. Although medical ecology holds no formal philosophy regarding nursing practice or medical practice and the care that each discipline gives to clients, the interdisciplinary findings from medical ecologists are being used as a supplemental instrument in recognizing the role of culture and the environment in relation to health and illness, and in developing theory. It is essential for today's health care provider to be cognizant of how environmental contamination compromises health. It is equally important to understand the world view of a particular culture and how that view can influence an individual's spiritual, emotional, and physical reactions to disease. It is also necessary to note how indigenous cultures differ from technological cultures when concerned with disease and individual reactions thereto.

The entire work is contextualized within and structured by theories of feminist methodology. We should recall that feminist methodology, positioned toward research on groups of women who were formerly ignored by social scientists (Reinharz, 1991, pp. 126–129), does not itself present an orthodoxy being outside the mainstream of investigation. In addition, the work embraces theories of phenomenology in which the "researcher seeks to understand the world of concerns . . . presented by the participant's narratives" (Benner, 1994, p. xiv), striving here to restore visibility to the voices of marginalized women.

Because of my history as a mixed blood woman who has ancestors in the circle of Jesuit and First Nations cultures, I am often accused of having enmity against the Jesuits and other patriarchal philosophies. This tone may season my writing from time to time. It is a phenomenon for which I *cannot* apologize.

Chapter 1

PERSONAL HISTORY
AND IMAGE

*I*n this chapter, I discuss the arrival of my ancestors to the North, who were members of First Nations People, the term now used to describe all tribes registered with the Canadian government. My experiences are linked with the experiences of the women whose stories are told here, through my heritage, my genetic link to breast cancer, and my fears of acquiring breast cancer. Healing begins with the telling of our stories.

A BRIEF OVERVIEW OF THE IROQUOIS AND HURON

First Nations People have persisted on this land for as long as collective memory. Initially hunter-gatherers, each cultural group of First Nations is distinct. Each trusts in its own creation myths, religion, social structure, sexual practices, clothing styles, baskets, and games. Linguistically, the bond is evident. Along the eastern woodlands and coastal areas, the Algonquin language links the cultures of First Nations People.

In September, the Canadian wilderness of the Huron and Iroquois people blushes with the brilliant colors of autumn. Although nightly frosts turn grasses and trees into colors of "spirits and ghosts," days linger crisp with brilliant sun and crystal-blue skies. Recognizing the harbinger of winter, the First People engage in a cycle of winter preparation. Understanding the natural systems and having respect for the land and animals, men hunt and fish. Women prepare meat, predominantly moose and deer, by drying or smoking. Tanning and smoking makes the hides supple so that they can be sewn into soft, warm clothing. Nothing is wasted. The bones are shaped into needles, weapons, and cooking utensils. In winter, the people move their bark wigwams inland away from coastal areas to winter camps, meadows where moose and caribou abound. During summer, women and children gather blueberries, fish, or hunt for small game such as birds and rabbits. Some cultures, such as the Iroquois, cultivate corn and squash. Diseases such as measles, whooping cough, smallpox, and influenza are unknown to the First People. This is as it was before contact with the Europeans; it was the cycle of life before contact with the Jesuits.

Quebec, 1650–?: Eustache Lambert

On September 17, 1650, twenty-year-old Eustache Lambert set sail from Bologne for the New World and what we know as Canada. He is my first ancestor from Europe who traveled to the New World. Leaving his mother and sister in the care of Urseline nuns, he enlisted as a *donne* with the Jesuit missionary, Isaac Jogues. The life of a donne was that of an indentured servant or lay missionary. What forces and courage urged Eustache on to his excursion in the New World, I will never know, but the adventure took him to the banks of the St. Lawrence River and to the villages of the Huron People. There are no records of Eustache's failures or achievements among the Huron of New France. Thwaites (1896–1901) notes that Eustache was an excellent rifleman, swordsman, and interpreter and from the diaries of others we can imagine life on the river as he traveled through the dark oak and pine forests of what is now modern Canada.

After two years of service, Eustache completed his work with the Jesuits and was given a grant of land along the St. Lawrence River in a signeural community called Lauzon. Eustache's cabin was situated on the bank of the river and became a favorite meeting place for the Indians on their way to Quebec.

His thirst for adventure characterizes many of his decendents and is reflected in my life and my brother's. My father, a direct descendent of Eustache, died of metastatic prostate cancer in 1989. When I visited him in the hospital, he was in a coma. As father and daughter we had a stormy relationship. I wanted to cry out to him to tell him that I loved him. I couldn't do anything except repeat, "Dad, Dad." As his vacant face turned to mine in a toothless, drooling gape, I wondered if his cancer-ridden brain processed anything I said. He will never know the words he needed to hear or the words I wanted to say.

Cocagne, New Brunswick, 1767–?:
Petit Francois Arsenault

Petit, the first known relative on my mother's side of the family, may have been descended from the Micmac chief and shaman, L'Kimu. From the writings of Mallard (1863) the name, Arguimeau (a translation of L'Kimu), is one of the earliest spellings of Arsenault. He is a descendent of Pierre Arguimeau. His home in Baie Verte was a gathering place for the people in the village where the American war with the British was discussed. A young donne named Joseph Gogeun, who was the assistant to the Jesuit missionary, Abbe Menache, lodged with Petit and his family in Baie Verte. Menache was sent by the Jesuits to provide "spiritual comfort" to the Micmac Indians and the Acadians. Joseph eventually married Petit's daughter, Anne.

When the British took Prince Edward Island in Canada during the American Revolution, the Acadians had long been a hunted people. In 1755, some five thousand Acadians were forcibly loaded onto deportation vessels for expulsion from their lands south into what is now America, many of whom, including those who escaped the British, settling in Louisiana. In 1760, Petit Francois Arsenault, his family and a handful of others, escaped to the coast of the Miramachi River in New Brunswick. During a severe winter and early frost, crops failed and the people endured cold and starving. It is said that the snow was six feet high. Many died including three of Petit's children (Hebert, undated). As a man of strength in adversity, Petit displayed many fine qualities that have been passed on to his future generations. His ability to take risks strengthened the adventurous spirit that Eustache gave us. And because of Petit, we are a gregarious family who carry within us a deep undying love of the sea.

New Brunswick, 1841–?: Domithilde Gogeun

During the years just before the American Revolution, the Micmac People of Canada were in a terrible state. Because many of their men were killed in the war, the women had no one to hunt for them and were reduced to begging. There was no food. Blankets were scarce. Because of measles, whooping cough, tuberculosis, and smallpox, all introduced by European colonists, the people were decimated (Paul, 1994). Today, Micmac people feel that because of imported disease and British racism, and no practical means of support, the Micmac were almost exterminated (Paul, 1994). It was into these meager times of hardship that my Micmac grandmother, Domithilde, was born in Cocagne, New Brunswick, on December 24, 1841. It is amazing that Domithilde lived at all considering the hardship affecting her people, but she was a strong infant.

In 1841, and recognizing the desperation of his people, even in fact to save them, the Grand Chief of the Micmac, Pemmeenaument, requested help from the British through a letter to Queen Victoria. Britain responded favorably—if slowly. Almost two years later in 1842, Britain passed the Indian Education and Permanent Resettlement Act which returned tribal land taken by Britain (Paul, 1994). Twenty-five years later, in 1867, when Canada became a confederation, the Micmac population had risen to 2000. It was at about this time that Domithilde fell in love with Germain Arsenault, a Frenchman. If she married him, a White man, under the Indian Act passed by the Canadian government, she would be considered a "non-status Indian" and lose her native rights. Perhaps because of economic conditions, it was not uncommon in those days for an Indian woman to marry a White man. There are no records of how they met or fell in love. Nor are there written diaries of family oppositions to the union. So, Domithilde, whatever her reasons, married Germain Arsenault and within a few years gave birth to my greatgrandfather, Calixte Arsenault. Domithilde was ninety-eight when she died and still walked three miles every Sunday to attend the Catholic Mass. I witnessed a brief second of her life in the nineteenth century as her life connects with mine through a yellowed, wrinkled photograph. In a long, black, Victorian-style skirt and starched white blouse, her smile is one of wisdom and gentleness. Domithilde's eyes mirror my own spark of independence.

Cocagne, New Brunswick, 18??–1936: Calixte Arsenault

Although he died before I was born, Calixte Arsenault was known by many of my aunts to be a stubborn old man who stole their candy. He married my greatgrandmother, Leda. In a formal photograph taken on their wedding day, Calixte appears as a handsome man with thick, light colored hair, gentle eyes, and a dimpled chin. His hand rests on my greatgrandmother's hand. They look very much in love. Calixte's dimple has not been lost to time as I carry it in my own chin as a remembrance of his stubborn character and those long-ago people.

Riviere De Loupe, New Brunswick, 1860–1953:
Leda Roi Arsenault

I can still see my greatgrandmother wearing her wine-colored dress. As I reflect on our lives, I am fortunate to have shared her life, listened to her stories, and enhanced the knowledge of our family's history. After dinner on Sundays, the women and my cousins and I would gather in the dining room. The older women—mothers, grandmothers, and aunts—would drink tea as they gossiped around the heavy Victorian mahogany table. Sometimes Aunt Ida would predict our future in the shapes of tea leaves at the bottom of our bone china cups. But my greatgrandmother, we called her Memere, which is probably a bastardization of the French *ma mere* [my mother], would gather us around her. As we sat on the window seat and over the dining room floor, Memere would tell us in French of the adventures of Tom Thumb. If I close my eyes, I can feel their spirits and visualize all of us gathered there. Many of the stories she told us came from her imagination; she was widely known as a creative story teller. Through her stories, Memere linked her past to our future. We would listen with rapt attention to stories about her "boys" when they fought in the war in France (World War I) or stories of Canada and "The Indians." Leda's mother, Demerise Gagnon Roi, is the first of my grandmothers who is known to have died of breast cancer. Eventually, Leda saw all of her sisters die from breast cancer. As a child, I knew these women as aged aunts, but in dusty, photograph albums I have seen faded tintypes of their bright, shining adolescent faces in the 1890s—beautiful round cheeked girls with narrow waists in crisp, cotton blouses: Rose, Ida, Helen (Leda's twin sister), Sarah, and Derilda. My memere gave me my middle name, Anne, for St. Anne, patron saint of the Micmac people and French Canadians. Memere said it was Saint Anne who protected her against breast cancer.

Amesbury, Massachusetts, 1898–1969:
George Dewey Arsenault

Perhaps because of his Micmac heritage or the fact that he spent much of his work day indoors, my grandfather always made time for us to share his love and knowledge of the natural world. I attribute my skill as a naturalist to his early influence. He would take my brother and me for long walks in the woods along the Charles River in Boston. He drew us simple "treasure maps" that we learned to use with skill. Sometimes the map took us to the edge of the forest or to the "creaking tree" where we would walk ten paces to find the treasure. Sometimes the treasure would be a buried acorn or a dime, or sometimes, candy.

He taught us to fish for catfish, to thread the worms on the hook with skill, not like a sissy, and to be wary of the barbels on the catfish's chin. I loved the feeling of pride that he showed me when I would catch those fish. I loved to honor his teaching by being the best fisherman in my family.

My grandfather never told stories of his war experiences in France, but one Sunday afternoon, during one of our family's get-togethers, he dug out his old World War I helmet. It was painted white with a great red A in the front. He told us that a German prisoner had painted it for him. This was no ordinary helmet. It was a great toy with which my cousins, brother, and I used to play the "Spinner" game. The head part with its leather straps was a perfect seat and I would spin around and around in Grandpa's helmet with my long braids twirling about trying to catch up with my head.

My grandfather was always with children. He honored them by his touch and the sound of his voice. When I grew up and moved away he adopted other neighborhood children and played "hocus pokus" or "find the treasure." My brother was with him in California when he died of lung cancer. He had become thin and frail with skin the color of brass. His love of life and the natural world has been my greatest gift.

A DEADLY LEGACY

These ancient ancestors have linked my future to their past by their stories, their love of freedom and nature, and their adventurous spirit. But somewhere within my family genes hides a deadly, defective chromosome called Chromosome 19. It controls the growth of the cell. Its defect passes on to each succeeding generation the predisposition to cancer—to breast cancer. Today, there are genetic and blood tests to discover the defect. I am too afraid to know. But these are some of the images and stories that preserve my individual heritage, honor, and give voice to my now quiet ancestors.

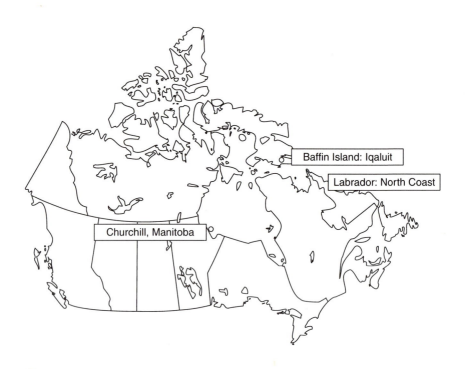

Baffin Island: Iqaluit

Labrador: North Coast

Churchill, Manitoba

Chapter 2

IMAGE OF WOMEN IN TRADITIONAL CULTURES

*I*n the far north of the Canadian and Alaskan wilderness lies the vast tundra. It is the land of the Northern Native People with whom my adventures and experiences gave balance to my life. My connection with this land is spiritual and seems to have no rational explanation. I am drawn to the North, to a unique ecosystem with its biodiversity of plants and animals, and to the rugged individuals who live there. As a mixed blood woman, perhaps my spiritual connection is also a genetic connection given to me as a gift through the adventurous spirits of my first ancestors and linked to the Native Peoples of Canada.

In the worldview of traditional people living in the North, it is critical to note how women develop images of themselves. In this chapter, I discuss the role of women in traditional cultures before European contact. It is important to note the traditional images of Native Women as an historical link to the women who tell us their stories in Chapter 4.

How do Native Women develop their own images? Some image development evolves from relationships within the family. How mothers relate to daughters and fathers relate to daughters evokes one image. How brothers relate to sisters may elicit another image. Today, some image development is linked to the media through advertising on television and in magazines. In most cases, images of women are culturally determined, now as then. For Northern Native Women, contact with the Catholic Church, particularly the

Jesuits, was instrumental in changing the traditional image First Nations women had of themselves.

Leading archeologists feel that northern populations, including Inuit, Inupiat, Athabascans, and other groups, migrated over 10,000 years ago from Siberia across a sea of grass known as Beringia and the Bering land bridge between Alaska and Russia (Chance, 1990). One may hear the term "Eskimo" used to describe the coastal people. Meaning eaters of raw fish/meat, Eskimo is derogatory and a designation first used by the Indian people, then by the first White people in the North. The people themselves prefer the name *Inuit* to designate indigenous people of the eastern Canadian Arctic. Those of the Bering Strait region prefer to be called Yup'ik, and those of the North Slope of Alaska are the Inupiat (Norman, 1990). When translated, these words mean "The First People." Indians and Inuit/Inupiat, however, are not of the same race of people.

In the traditional view of many Northern Native People, Raven, the Creator and Trickster, created the first human:

After creating light and water for the world, Raven decided to make the first creature for his world. We call that creature "man." Because Raven had no experience at making man, he created the first man out of rocks, but the man was too slow and heavy. Then Raven thought of making a man out of sticks, but this man didn't suit Raven at all. Then he thought of making man out of leaves and that is what Raven did. Leaves die and fall in the winter and so man also dies.

After Raven made the first man, he taught him lots of tricks and about war (Salisbury, 1983), but these are stories reserved for cold winter nights in the Singing House.*

Volumes are written about the adventures of male explorers and whalers in the Arctic. But with respect to the role of the Northern Native Women and how their survival skills in northern environments aided the European explorers and whalers, written information is limited. As in the past, today's Northern Native Women are especially resourceful in finding food sources, delivering babies, and contributing as members of their culture. Inuit women who are over fifty years old remember what life was like

---

*Singing House: a communal gathering place for the Inuit where stories and songs help to pass the long winter nights.

in the early camps before the government brought the Inuit into settlements in the 1960s. A woman's role was well-defined then and the images that Inuit women had of themselves came from their skills as hide skinners, clothing makers, cooks, healers, shamen, story tellers, or carvers. Women were valued for their skills which could mean "life or death for their man or family caught in an arctic emergency" (Billson, 1988).

Women were supposed to take care of the home. A man does the hunting. A woman takes care of the kids and the food. She should know how much they got left; how much food there is for the kids. They always check the food. The woman always sews or patches the clothes for the husband and the kids. She also scrapes all the skins, caribou, seal or whatever skins there is . . . the man never cooks or feeds the kids because he is out hunting all day. Women go up the river to hunt ptarmigan while the men are hunting caribou (From a conversation with an elder from Barrow: Chance, 1990, p. 112).

Billson (1995) indicates that the social stratification of the Inuit community is changing as are the roles of Inuit men and women. Today, Inuit women work as teachers, nurses, social workers, and clerks. Their work has become their lifeline in the cash economy of the modern North. As a result, the role of these women appears more stressful, more difficult, and more thankless. The economic necessity for women to work outside the home is greater, and yet there is still the responsibility of keeping the family together. As a result, women are taking more control of their own lives: for example, when to marry, when to start a family, and how to get an education (Crnkovich, 1988, p. 61).

THE INUPIAT

In Alaska, the counterpart of the Canadian Inuit are called *Inupiat*. To non-natives, they are descendants of the first migration wave across the Bering Land Bridge over 10,000 years ago, but like the Inuit and others of the North, their view of creation is shrouded in myths of Sedna,* sea goddesses, and Raven:

---

*Sedna: in Inuit/Inupiat mythology: Sedna's father was going to marry her to someone that Sedna didn't love. One day while in her father's canoe, she tried to escape. But as she did so, he cut off her fingers which then became the creatures of the sea.

For hundreds of years, the Inupiat of Arctic Alaska lived in distinct, territorial based populations scattered along the coast of Alaska. Highly competent, they had [and continue to have] an intimate knowledge of their environment. (Chance, 1990, p. 29)

A flexible division of labor among youths was clearly recognized by the Inupiat. Women and girls went hunting and fishing. Boys were often responsible for cleaning the house and helping with cooking. Men and women assumed responsibility in both spheres (Chance, 1990).

Although distinct characteristics concerning the roles of men and women define the variety of cultures and tribes, generally in all tribes men were the hunters. Their weapons, harpoons, spears, knives, and so on, often held religious significance and power to aid them in taking an animal's life. If weapons were unclean or contaminated by the touch or essence of a menstruating woman, for example, the animals were dishonored and would not give themselves to the hunters. Many cultures also believed that when women were in their "moon time" they held the greatest power. Taboos evolved around the blood of women. It was taboo for menstruating women to touch a hunter's weapons, to serve him food, or to be in the same room as the hunter. So it evolved in many traditional cultures of the North that menstruating women were set apart from the rest of the community, segregated in their menstrual hut, forbidden to join celebrations or mingle with hunters for fear of contaminating weapons or offending animal spirits (Neithammer, 1977). Countless traditional tribal people maintain this belief and menstruating women continue to be barred from participating in ceremonies even today.

When her "moon time" was over, there were prescribed cleansing rituals that had to be followed, including bathing in cold stream water, smudging, and eating special foods. Similar customs characterized the menstruating women of the Inuit culture as well. Although the traditions seem harsh, many women welcomed the monthly relief from household duties and demanding husbands (Neithammer, 1977).

For their part, Haida women cooked food in pit ovens dug into the ground. Intricate baskets were made using materials of red and yellow cedar and spruce roots. Cloth for ceremonial robes was woven from mountain goat wool, dog wool, and in some cases, bird down. Men worked in wood and in stone. The Haida and Tsimshian people inherited their place in society from their mothers. Women in these two northwest coastal groups held a higher status than women whose line came from their fathers. Both men and women could be shamen. Women were the bearers of children and kept the family supplied with meat by hunting close to home when the men were on extended hunting trips. Elder women rather than elder men were regarded as great "Keepers of the Wisdom" (Conrad, 1993).

Among the Haida and many other tribes of the northwest coast, northern interior, and Alaska, Raven myths are prominent. But Raven, who was considered both Creator and Trickster, certainly was not alone. Other important animals include the bear as a nexus for power, the wolf for intelligence and strength, the otter for play and healing, and the thunderbird (eagle) who was seen as a fellow hunter. Whether taken alone or ensemble, all were incredibly formidable presences within tribal life. As animal spirits they influenced human affairs (Langdon, 1993; Nelson, 1983). Celebrations called Potlatches* were also given to honor weddings, deaths, naming of children, or to demonstrate a clan's high status (Langdon, 1991).

First Nations Women in Canada

There are many many tribes and bands that comprise the First Nations of Canada; they differ from one another in language, customs, and laws.

Unfortunately, for much of the culture of the eastern woodland tribes, including the Micmac and the Malaseet, contact with Europeans ended in disaster, with much priceless history either suppressed or obliterated. Today, most tribes are learning to reestablish elements of their culture that were lost to colonialism and to relearn forgotten languages and customs. In this work, I have taken the liberty to present a brief overview of First Nations' People. For tribes which are not included in this overview, I apologize.

In pre-contact Canada, native societies were organized around hunting, fishing, and gathering. Some were predominantly horticultural societies, as the Iroquois people of the St. Lawrence River valley, who grew squash, corn, and beans. As with many Indian cultures, the children of

---

*Potlatch: A celebratory feast which takes months or even years to prepare the gifts, the food and the dancers. The host gives away all of his possessions to the guests. More about this important celebration can be found in the glossary.

the Iroquois descended from their mother's family line. The woman owned the home. Men who married Iroquois women went to live in the "woman's dwelling." Should the couple separate or divorce, the man must leave the home, since it was owned by the woman. The women were also the main food producers and accomplished all of the agricultural work (Conrad, 1993). Although divorce protocols differed from tribe to tribe, generally divorce was common and easily accomplished. A woman took her children and possessions, left the husband, and went to live with her parents. If the woman owned the home, the man was ejected along with his possessions (Neithammer, 1977).

In learning the roles of women, young Indian girls built toy villages complete with teepees, real household utensils, and played house. When moving to a new winter camp or fish camp, the girls packed up and moved their tiny villages just as the grown-up women moved the adult camp. Girls learned their skills by watching and playing and were further educated by observing their aunts, grandmothers, or older sisters. In many matrilineal and matrilocal tribes, the word for *mother* and *aunt* was often the same word (Neithammer, 1977).

Ojibwa women remained close to home when their men went hunting. The women were important intermediaries between the spirit world and the people. Often regarded as great healers, the women also cleaned the wigwams and maintained family life (Conrad, 1993). A Sioux woman presided over the Sun Dance Ceremony* held among the Plains Indians of southern Canada and northern United States, the woman's extended family promising to publicly sponsor the event in the name of a male relative whose life was in danger (Conrad, 1993).

---

*Sun Dance: Evidence by anthropologists suggest that the Sun Dance was invented by the Plains Algonquins as early as 1700. From the eighteenth to the nineteenth century, the Sun Dance Ceremony was the grandest of all religious ceremonies performed. Before the dancing began, the Sun Dance chief, who received a vision to direct the dance, selected a center pole to erect which was then surrounded by 10 other poles to define the boundaries of the dance. After Christianity came to the Plains Algonquins, the poles were increased to 12 to symbolize the 12 Apostles. Singers and drummers sat in the southeast portion of the circle made by the poles. In the center, the men danced for three days without food or water (today, women also dance). When the dancers fell, it was said that they were receiving their vision. They were administered to by the Sun Dance chiefs and his sub chiefs. The dancers received blessings from the shaman when the dancing was over. The dancers paid the shaman through gifts of shawls, blankets, horses and, in contemporary times, money. Following the dance a feast of buffalo and bread was served (Jorgenson, 1972).

Micmac women were widely known as excellent and creative weavers of mats, baskets, and bags. Learning these skills as a young girl through grandmother's stories or by visiting with aunties, a Micmac girl also learned the growing season for each plant and where to gather them. Knowing where to seek grasses, reeds, birch bark for healing, and how to build a wigwam brought honor to the Micmac woman as a valuable member of her culture. Spirit was also important to the Micmac people, who believed that souls could take the shapes of different bodies, usually animals, called spirit helpers. As a result, bears and other animal spirit helpers were called upon for strength in adversity. Micmac women were also respected as healers. They knew how to call upon the spirit helpers, how to set bones using an eel skin as an elastic bandage or birch bark splints, and how to use fir balsam as a healing salve for wounds. In addition, the women learned to make pottery using clay and sand mixed with the shells of marine mollusks (Whitehead, 1983). Within 100 years of European contact, however, 75 percent of the Micmac population was dead from European-introduced diseases (Whitehead, 1983).

When the Europeans arrived in New France, Jesuit missionaries accompanied them. Without regard or respect for the social structure of the Native people, the Jesuits attempted to impose European social values on them, and which included male authority, female fidelity. The Jesuits noted with disdain the equality of women among the Micmac, the Montagnais, and the other Algonquin tribes of northern Quebec and southern Labrador (Leacock, 1991). Among the Indian tribes of Canada, the women as well as the men had autonomy and this autonomy was central to the structure of society. One person was not considered better than another (Leacock, 1991). Rebelling against the Jesuit's teachings, however, the women continued to have lovers, practice bigamy, encourage married men to take a second wife, and to defy their Christian or recently converted husbands (Leacock, 1991).

In this chapter, I have attempted to provide a broad overview of women's images in traditional northern cultures—women's autonomous role and family life. The eroding of women's images began as a result of contact with Europeans and Jesuits. As we approach the twenty-first century, the image of Northern Native Women continues in transition, influenced by a clashing and blending of traditional cultures from the North and the technology-driven, cash economy culture of the South. It is an image and lifestyle that contributes to their worldview of health and illness.

Pangnirtunq Pass, Baffin Island, Arctic Canada—Lost Caribou Antler by Frank Tyro. Used with permission.

Chapter 3

THE IMAGE OF DISEASE, THE IMPACT OF BIOLOGY IN WESTERN CULTURE

*I*n this chapter, I discuss selected literature in which Caucasian women tell their personal stories, describing their images and experiences. Although I have never met the women whose lives are reviewed briefly here, I feel I have known them intimately through the lives and stories of the women in my family. Their stories of survival are stories that have been told by my grandmothers, aunts, and mother. Their stories may one day be my story. Unfortunately, the literature in which women discuss personal experiences with breast cancer is narrowly focused on White women. Aside from Audre Lorde's *Cancer Journals*, work describing the images of native women and women of color is largely unwritten. It is my hope that this book will help to correct a gross negligence.

Because of the many similarities in our lives, it is interesting to comment on Terry Tempest Williams' 1992 narration prior to reviewing several other stories. Williams is a Utah-born naturalist who works in the Great Bear Reserve near Salt Lake where she grew up. Both of us share a love of and a career in the natural world. Both of us share a family history of breast cancer. Williams is the oldest in a family of Mormons whose ancestors came to Utah in the 1880s seeking religious freedom. Her grandmother, Mimi, an ardent birder, and her mother, an outdoor enthusiast, fostered

Terry's love for the natural world and the land around the Great Salt Lake. In 1983, Terry learned that her family had been exposed to fallout from radiation as a result of nuclear testing in Nevada by the U.S. government. She realized that the government had deceived her; children were growing up drinking contaminated milk from contaminated cows; children were drinking milk from their mother's contaminated breasts. Terry believes that the breast cancer in her family is a result of the nuclear testing (Williams, 1991). Terry's mother, grandmother, and six aunts have all had mastectomies—seven are dead. (My mother, grandmother, five aunts, and three cousins have had mastectomies—five are dead.) Terry calls her family the "Clan of the One-Breasted Women." She watched helplessly as her mother underwent chemotherapy, lost her hair, and vomited for days on end. During the last stages of her mother's illness when she was confined to bed with a morphine drip, Terry dealt with the realization that her mother had only days to live. It was during this time that Terry wished for her grandmothers to help her. Terry turned to her family but felt betrayed in doing so. She then turned to her religion but fared no better. Her religion asked for unconditional love and obedience to the laws of God, which she refused. Her government asked for unconditional belief in their claims concerning the safety of nuclear testing and fallout, when much of what the government was telling the residents of Utah and Nevada was a lie.

Barbara Rosenblum, an assistant professor of sociology who died of breast cancer at forty-four, also wrote of feeling betrayed by her government and, at least initially, by her religion. Her cancer was misdiagnosed by experts at Kaiser Memorial Hospital in New York. Her mammogram was also misdiagnosed by the radiologists. No one was suspicious enough to do a needle biopsy even when one breast was one-and-a-half times the size of the other (Butler & Rosenblum, 1991). Barbara and her parents were city dwellers who relied on clinic medicine. She writes of never knowing what good medical treatment was and of being done in by shoddy medical practice. It is the same shoddy medical treatment that is being doled out to poor women even today. It is the politics of breast cancer. After three years of chemotherapy, vomiting, hair loss; after three years of radiation treatments, the breast cancer invaded Barbara's lungs and liver. When she knew she was dying, she gathered her friends around her in a support group. From these friends, her family ties, and her final return to Jewish religion, she sought the strength to sustain her through an agonizing death.

In the way the government, religion, and medicine responded to the dilemmas of these two women, the need for subordination—a structural attribute of patriarchal authority—is unmistakable. The use and common misuse of such authority has left much damage in its wake, both in regard to women's rights and women's health. And in Third World countries as well as in the United States it continues today (Shiva, 1993).

A number of other women have written accounts of their breast cancer experience. Ronnie Kaye (1991), for example, describes images of fear, anxiety, and isolation in dealing with testing, doctors, unfamiliar territory, coping with hospitals and surgery, tolerating treatments that can be devastating, and coming to terms with death. From it all, an image of powerlessness emerges for Kaye. For her part, Joyce Wadler (1992) notes that no one can know the stress of a positive mammogram. Today, after her surgery, however, she feels stronger and writes, with courage, that "death will come when it damn well pleases."

During and after her experience of breast cancer, Nancy Baker (1991) also depicts feelings of fear as well as images of lost female sexuality and feminity, lost peace of mind, feelings of being alone, and not having or not being able to easily confide in someone about her fears.

Suicide is another possibility that many women consider during or after their breast cancer experience. Metzger (1978), for one, describes her survival as an end to a nightmare. No longer fearful of making love or even of looking at herself in the mirror, she has become an "Amazon" with a fine red scar across her chest on which she has tattooed a tree. In her eyes, she owns the body of a warrior. She is a woman who has survived the trauma.

These stories, and so many more not mentioned here, stories that you the reader may know just as well as I, validate women's experiences as well as enabling communication among other women. The women's work is biographical as well as topical. The women's work allows us to hear their stories, to see the patterns of commonalities that breast cancer has brought to their lives.

Breast cancer can alter a woman's image of herself as a woman, as a sexual being, as a healthy woman. For White women, progress comes through a series of self-images motivated by disbelief, anxiety, fear, loss of womaness, of being an unworthy sexual partner, of hoping for a cure and a life, and of strength after survival. Once the issue of living with death is resolved, the rest of living evolves into an act of strength and humility, of experiencing joy in one more day of life. I wonder if it is the same for Northern Native Women?

Baffin Island, Arctic Canada—Abandoned Dog Sled. Photo by Frank Tyro. Used with permission.

Chapter 4

Breast Cancer Stories Told by Northern Native Women

*I*n this chapter, we hear the voices of Northern Native Women who have experienced breast cancer. Their stories transpire from many cultures across the North. Their stories respond to the question posed at the end of Chapter 3: "I wonder if it is the same for Northern Native Women?"

A Story from Churchill, Manitoba: Leah: 1989

Leah is the first Inuk [singular form of Inuit] I called friend. We came into one another's lives because we are teachers at the Northern Studies Centre, Churchill, Manitoba, "Polar Bear Capital of the World." Through an interpreter, Leah, an expert hide tanner of Inuit technique, was teaching caribou hide tanning to anthropologists from the Smithsonian Institution. I was teaching arctic ecology to a group of graduate students from Philadelphia. Every day Leah and I sat together for meals. I asked her to help me learn her language. She beams, "I teach you good." I am a sponge. I point to things on the table and Leah tells me in Inuktitut. I write down everything phonetically: *Nuyok*, hair; *EEEMY*, Oh Boy; *matna*, thank you. Leah is patient and, through her kindness, I come away knowing Inuktitut names for parts of the body, animals, dishes, and food. A chain smoker and bubble gum chewer, Leah validates descriptions of Inuit morphology described by Boas (1901) and others: short, barely five feet, chubby, and tanned. Her smile is endearing: we communicate through signs, a smattering of English, and the Inuktitut words that Leah teaches me. On the evening of our last night in Churchill, Leah and I and my class travel by van along the sluggish dirt road leading to Twin Lakes Overlook, two miles from the study center. Living in the arctic tundra habitat of Arviat, Northwest Territories, Leah's experience with the boreal forest is limited. As we bounce along the forest road in the van, she explains, *EEEMY* at the proliferation of spruce trees. She tells me she has 18 kids. I point to my genitalia and exclaim, *EEEMY*. We all laugh.

At the overlook, the students pile out of the van and scatter in all directions toward the lake and forest. They seek some last moments in the Arctic solitude. Leah gingerly lowers her stocky body into the sand and kneels to draw the tracks of animals. I sit cross-legged like a diligent child learning at grandmother's knee. Unhurriedly, in the sand along the edge of the lake, with both hands moving at once, she outlines the hind prints of a polar bear. "*Nanook,*" she whispers quietly. I clumsily draw a small white tailed deer print and Leah whispers, "*Baby Tuktu* (caribou)." We continue drawing tracks as the setting sun behind us transforms the colors of the sky and lake to red, orange, purple. Leah draws the track of a goose and reveals, "Good to eat." She explains in her language and with signs that Canada Goose is used as a food source, but Snow Goose is not. Tracks of other animals and birds are drawn. Stars are winking. In her melodious voice, Leah begins to sing a folk song in Inuktitut. Her village lays further north on Hudson Bay. We both will be leaving for home in the morning. We have become close friends. In the custom of learning from traditional women, I have shared her path and now understand much about her language and her culture. There is much more to know. "Lori Ikaki, be sad tomorrow when go in plane. I love you." We hug, both of us with tears in our eyes. We share a sadness knowing in our hearts we may never meet again. It is as a result of these cherished relationships with Northern Native People and my passion for northern ecosystems, the beauty of the land and culture, that I approach a path in my life where I am summoned on a journey to explore the North and Native Women's health.

STORIES FROM LABRADOR

To know the women, you must trust the land.

Labrador, a rocky country of 300,000 square miles of infertile soils supporting a population of 30,000, is located between Hudson Bay and the Labrador Sea. There are five basic cultural regions in Labrador, each with its own lifestyle and distinctive community. Labradorians divide the People of their country in the following way: 850 Naskapi/Montagnais Indians (The Innu Nation), 1500 Inuit, and 10,000 settlers of European descent who came to Labrador in the 1700s–1800s. These stories are focused on the North coast among the Inuit and the settlers.

For three hundred years, the Labrador Sea, one of the richest fishing grounds in the world, was known for its flourishing codfish industry. Until 1959 the entire fishing industry took place inshore. Then, in 1959, the offshore spawning banks were located and deliberately depleted by foreign fishing vessels. The economy of Labrador was changed forever. Where once the sea supported 20,000 fishermen, today there is a moratorium on codfish fishing and the sea supports no one. Catches by European trawler fleets using electronic sensors peaked at over 800,000 tons, nearly six times the inshore harvest (Petro-Canada, 1975). As a result of the depletion and moratorium, the native people are angry at the government for not intervening on their behalf; they go hungry and lose income. In the vastness that is Labrador, too, there is no mammography available to women. The government is concerned with the fishing industry and it appears that they have no time for "women's business."

Labrador: Journal Entry

As I prepare to research in Labrador, my mother is also dying from her breast cancer. I will refer to my field journal from time to time as this narration unfolds.

12/19/93   I am gathering my things for the Labrador trip. My Northface backpack is filled with Arctic gear: long johns, sweaters, boots, and my gortex Antarctica jacket. Whenever I wear it I feel close to other arctic explorers. Gifts of tea and honey for the women are carefully packed. These things are brought to the women as something of myself. I include two cameras, camcorder, tapes, pencils, and other writing paraphanelia. My phone calls home to speak with my mother and my grandmother are links to our past history with breast cancer and my future. The women in my family are the special connections. They gather me in for special occasions; they release me in freedom of pursuit.

12/28/93   I am on the way to Montreal at last! The women in the seats behind me speak to one another in French. If I close my eyes, I am transported 30 years into the past, to Sunday afternoons with my greatgrandmother's family gathered around the dining table sharing tea, *les peitis gateaux,* and coffee. They are telling stories. Aunt Ida is telling fortunes and futures in the tea leaves at the bottom of our empty tea cups. She never predicted breast cancer.

From Philadelphia it is an eleven hour journey to Labrador. I fly the last leg of the journey in a lumbering old Dash 8 hanging in freezing rain and blackened sky. My thoughts are random. I think about my mother in her darkened room, vomiting, drinking, and in denial about her possible metasticies. I worry about her failed kidneys filled with stones, dehydration, and cancer cells invading her liver and bones. I think about the women I am about to meet. I'll never see their dying. Will it be like mine? Like Mom's? I think about my own mortality and death. It frightens me.

12/29/93   Goose Bay at last!

The day dawns with crisp brilliant blue skies and pale, yellow sun. It is biting cold, minus 58 degrees Fahrenheit. My nasal passages feel like cardboard. We have clambered aboard the Twin Otter and are ready for the trip up the North coast of Labrador. The Twin Otter, symbol of air travel in the North, carries 18 passengers: no frills, no bathroom air travel. After pulling in the rickety stairs on his way to the cockpit, the co-pilot instructs us to read the emergency card and to fasten the seat belt. For its size and payload, the Twin Otter is remarkably graceful—like a small hawk. Inside, the seats are filled with holiday travelers bundled up in parkas. Their breathing and body heat carries condensation to the windows. We fly along the coast at 17,000 feet, the endless sea of Sedna frozen in waves on one side and Raven's forest on the other. Below, a quilt of ice and snow covers the rugged, desolate land. Bears and other hibernators sleep in their dens, unaware of winter. Seed and insect eating birds have flown south to more abundant food supplies. Here and there, caribou are running among frozen spruce forest meadows. Their long legs and wide hooves are especially adapted for long-distance Arctic travel. The silvery wolf remains hidden and elusive, its acute hearing and sense of smell eternally in pursuit of voles, shrews, and bigger game. Rolling mountains, dense, dark forest, and frozen lakes penetrate every direction. It is *the glorious North!*

THE STORIES

Labrador, The North Coast, 1993: Mimi

Halfway up the north coast, the Twin Otter circles Mimi's tiny village nestled amidst spruce forest and frozen sea. From the air, skiddo tracks can be seen crisscrossing until they disappear under the shadows of the dark, dense forest. It appears as a holiday village in miniature set out on artificial snow. As the pilot gets the tail-wind, we land on the snow encrusted, gravel airstrip and embark to a hulking mass of curious friends and relatives all jostling for greeting space at the foot of the shaky steps. Their breath condenses in a great massive cloud. The side baggage door is thrown open and gear tossed out to the scrambling crowd. A rugged old man with piercing blue eyes driving a skiddo informs me that he will take me from the airstrip to the bed and breakfast where a meeting with Mimi and her husband has been arranged. I am thankful for my gortex parka and fur ruff as we speed down the mountainside to the village. The air temperature is minus 56 degrees and, with the velocity of the skiddo, I can't imagine the wind chill. My cheeks turn crimson in the twenty minutes it takes to reach the village, but my body temperature is warm.

When she arrives at the bed and breakfast, I am amazed to see how tiny Mimi is. Wearing seal skin *kamiks* [boots] and dressed in a warm parka, she appears as an old apple head doll. A scarf of Russian design, red roses on a dark blue background, is wrapped about her head. Her life as a trapper's wife has taken its toll. I look into her smiling, weather-worn face, "I am honored that you would talk to me." With her actions and warmth in her voice, she treats me like a member of her own family. "I likes lookin' at you, girl. I thought you'd be older, and fat with short hair," she says, laughing. "I thought you'd be a little old Inuk lady." We both laugh, because she is. We travel by skiddo around her settlement. She is eager for me to know the places she feels are important: the old salt box house where she was born, unoccupied, and badly in need of paint. The old boards, worn by storms and blizzards that lash out on this rugged coastal land, are icons of the people who call this place home—rugged, weather-worn but strong. (Mimi's husband, a hunter has shot six caribou that morning and has given them all away to people who have no one to hunt for them, perpetuating the Inuit ideal of helping one another.) I sit in the bottom of the *komatik** [sometimes spelled kamotik] box amidst frozen snow turned pink from the caribou blood and imagine caribou running in the forest.

Because Mimi's husband is a fisherman in the summer, he is eager for us to see his boat, "named after my two granddaughters," he says, proudly. That night I am invited to a wedding at the Moravian Church. "The whole town will be there, you come too," Mimi announces. I am honored.

Later that evening B_____ drives us to the church in his komatik box and skiddo. The white, wooden Moravian church, snuggled into a blanket of snow, is decorated for Christmas with candles and evergreens. Other people arrive on their skiddos. The smell of gas fills the night air. Inside, the Moravian star hangs from the ceiling in front of an altar where beeswax candles burn quietly. Soon, the little church is filled with song; they are familiar Moravian hymns I recognize from Vesper Service at Moravian College, Bethlehem, Pennsylvania. It is comforting to listen and join in song with Inuit voices and faces so far away from home.

Mimi and B_____'s happy house is decorated for Christmas. A towering spruce tree cut in the nearby forest sits majestically in the corner of their spacious living room. Its pine scent fills the room. Gaily wrapped gifts flow out from beneath. Tiny, white crocheted stars, trees, and snow flakes decorate the branches. It is obvious that because of her husband's prowess as a hunter and fisherman, they have a good life. B_____, an excellent hunter, provides well for his family. His skill as a hunter also helps support other families. Their house with six bedrooms, one for each of their children, was built by B_____'s own hand. The warm, yellow, kitchen is the most spacious room in the house with a large inviting, table, bench, and welcome for all who enter.

---

*Komatik box: A long box made of wood that fits on the sled. It is used to carry wood, animals, people, etc.

Mimi used her special china and flatware to serve us tea and cakes. Her granddaughter told us that we must be special because she never uses them unless someone special is the guest. I watch Mimi as she carefully unwraps the spoons from a special tin in her bedroom. In the same tin with her special tea things is Mimi's Moravian Church hat. She reverently takes off the tissue that wraps a delicately crocheted lace oval with blue ribbons that tie under the chin. She proudly tells me about the custom that Moravian women in Labrador have kept since the early days of the Moravian Church. "Up there in Nain the girls and boys sit separate from one another in Church. The girls wear a Church-hat—of crocheted white wool for winter, lace for summer—blue ribbons for married women, pink for unmarried, white for widows. I don't go to Church without my hat." I should have taken a photo of the hat.

Breathtaking picture windows overlook a magnificent view of their settlement. Family photos are everywhere and they eagerly show us the other members of their family: Her husband's brother paralyzed from the waist down with polio, Mimi as a child on her mother's knee, an assortment of their children. Family kinships are meaningful.

Mimi's Story   The Moravian Missions founded this settlement before the Hudson's Bay Company came. There were only two families here then in them days, my grandfather and another family.

> The history of M_____ is not the oldest settlement on the Labrador coast. . . . M_____ began in 1896 when the Moravian Mission came to lead the Eskimos to the Faith in Jesus. The settlement now boasts 329 people; 140 are Eskimo. The Moravian Mission house was prefabricated in Germany and shipped to Labrador on the mission boat. A small hospital serving two or three patients was built in M_____ as well as the boarding school. (Saunders, 1983)

I was born in that little old house. There were no nurses here in them days so my grandmother helped my Mum when I was born. I have eleven in the whole family. The earliest memory I have is of my father's death. He was coming home from the woods on Christmas Eve, out getting our tree and looking at his traps with his komatik and sled dogs when he fell through the ice and drowned. Uncle Bill took me home because we didn't have any heat or water at our house. But, my mother put me there with Uncle Bill. She made me go and live with his family so they could take care of me. We used to go to the summer place by the boat near the bay. We used to cut the fish. They were codfish in them days. We used to go pick bake apples [cloud berries] and other berries too. I had a job at the Moravian Mission cleaning house, scrubbing on the floor with a brush and doing the wash on the wash board. That kind of thing. Uncle Bill took me to that job. The parents used to bring the kids up to the school at the Moravian Mission. I went to school. Not long, but not long enough to learn. I was too stubborn, I guess.

I knows how to sew the boots from seal skins, but I cleaned my first skin when I was fifty. I used to make the boots for my kids when I was younger, in my twenties, but I got the skins cleaned from someone else. I cleaned the skins with a board and a pan, and put the board in the pan and use the *ulu** to clean the skin. It was good for my arm, eh. We used to hunt the seals in the spring. We used to eat the seals once in a while and give it to our dogs too. Now we have chickens from the [supply] boat.

When we was growing up, we used to eat caribou, rabbits, fish, partridges, we never ate whales, but we ate "jumpers."† The jumpers are awful good meat. We used to shoot 'em with a gun, not with a harpoon. We had so much fish here in them days you could put a bucket down with a stone and the fish would just go in. There's no more cod here now. . . . from overfishing from the foreign boats. It makes me mad. No one was there to tell the boats to stop. Now we have no more codfish here.

I was 13 when I had my first period. There was an old lady. Her name was Aunt Bertha. She taught me and another girl about being a woman and all. She told me that "Something is going to poke you in your green place [where things grow]."

Aunt Bertha was the local midwife on that part of the Labrador coast. She was known as Aunt Bertha by everyone from Rigolet to Nain. She would travel to Nain by dogsled to deliver a baby for one of the missionaries or travel to Hudson Bay post at Rigolet. She never lost one case of child birth and would take no money for her services. Aunt Bertha had no medical training and was a good hunter and trapper. (Chard, 1978)

---

*Ulu: Inuit woman's knife with a curved blade. The attachment and design of the handle varies from village to village.

†Jumpers: A local word meaning dolphin or porpoise.

I was 19 when I had my first child, that's John, and my last child at 32, that's Tommy. I have it all written down in the bible. John is the one who carves. Dr. Paddon was here in them days. I wasn't scared. I just said to Susie, my friend, "I think I'm sick. I wonder how many hours am I still to live?" B_____ [her husband] was there.

My sister had cancer. She died of cancer and my brother Jim also had cancer. He died. I held him until the last and he died. He said, "You come see me [in the hospital]." I said, "I'm coming back to see you after dinner." He said, "You don't have to." It was 11:30 when I came back and he was already dead. He used to be sick all the time. Back and forth to the hospital to St. Anthony and back again. He died of cancer of the stomach. My brother Bob stayed with Jim all summer while he was sick.

One morning I woke up, but I wasn't feeling like there was anything wrong, and I put my hand up between my breasts and felt the lump. It was like a hen's egg. I said to B_____ "I got a lump on my breast." and B told me to go right down to the nurse. She said, "You have to have a check up." So I went to Goose Bay and then to St. Anthony [Newfoundland]. And that's where I had my surgery and my X-rays. The doctor took the biopsy and there was nothing wrong on the first piece [of tissue], so he took the whole thing [tumor] and when it came back [from the lab] he told me I had cancer. I felt like I didn't know what to say or what to do. He told me it would be better to go home to my family first [before the mastectomy]. He told me I had to have my breast removed. I cried real soft when I heard about it. I was thinking of my kids and my home. I said to Dr. Fitz, I thought when I came back, my kids would catch it. So I came back and said goodbye to my kids. I must say, it was hard. B_____ came out after I was there in St. Anthony's. I felt like I was going to die at first. "How many years do I have to live?" I asked him. "I asked the Doctor and he said he didn't know there are no guarantees," B_____ responded. "If I could live two years, eh. I want to see my kids get bigger," I said. That was in 1977. I had to fight with myself. I stayed in St. Anthony's a month and I had cobalt treatment in St. John's. B_____ would make me eat. All I wanted to do was sleep. I was 49. If he didn't keep me up, I would have given up. Then I met someone who had both breasts off. "Don't feel bad, you haven't got two. I just had both of mine off," she said. She lifted me up. I talked to other women. Then I talked to Aunt Lilly. I talked to she a lot. I felt that part of my womaness was gone. But I don't feel that now. B_____ loved me through the whole thing. It was like it didn't bother him. He just wanted me. I found out that I am more valuable than my breast. B_____ was OK the first time we made love too. It was like he didn't mind.

I would tell other women to try to fight for themselves; fight for their life. It is so hard, though, but with God's help they will get through. It made me stronger that I could fight. There is nothing now that I'm scared of. Before I was scared of everything; and if things happen to me now, like if my blood pressure goes up, I'm not scared, eh. I want to hold you again. I need to hold your hand. [We both get caught up emotionally in her story and we stop to have a cup of tea. I mentally review my mother's breast cancer experience and the sadness that we as a family felt as a result of my mother's loss.]

We need a good cry once in a while. It makes me feel better. We need to talk about it [having breasts removed]. It makes me feel good to talk about it, because B_____ won't . . . won't talk about it with me.

During the tea break, Mimi asks, "How do people get breast cancer?" I think about how to answer this question to a woman who is unable to read or write or know about genetics. "Sometimes it is in your family's blood line, [meaning genetic]. Sometimes it can come from pollution." Albert, her husband, nods at my answer. He understands pollution of the fish and the land. I continue, "Sometimes if your mother or grandmother has it [genetically], it will come to you too." I see understanding on Mimi's face, she knows about cancer in her brother and her sister.

When I was in the hospital I wondered if I was ever going to come out of here and I heard something speak to me. One morning I was in the isolation for a week because I had an infection. That morning I woke up and I wasn't feeling very good; I had a wash and when I got in the bed I wanted to just give up, "I'll never get out of here," I said to myself, "I got to get out." I heard my name, eh. Something spoke to me, and said, "You got a good soul there; you got a good soul, like your spirit there, just look up." There was a big shiny ball rolling around the ceiling of the ward. It spoke to me and I jumped right up to look at the ball. After that I was OK. When I come back I called the nurse and she told me that is just what I needed to see. I thought that it might have been my head, eh. The ball was rolling around. It was a shiny light. I think that it must have been from heaven. The voice said that I'd be alright. I went through a lot, but still, I'm alright now. I prayed a lot.

The souls were essential to Inuit philosophy and psychology, encouraging exploration for strengths of character within the name soul. Name souls were guardians and floated freely above the cosmos and possessed strength of mind and character. The name soul was not only within the individual, but also invisible without. (Minor: 1992, pp. 37–39)

B_____ made me eat oranges, applies, and all the fruit. It was different from my home food, but there was nothing wrong with it. I never took special medicine teas or plants. I had my last coffee when I come back in '77. It just turned me off when I had my last cobalt treatment. I drinks tea now. It's just the same. I wouldn't change anything what I had done to me in the hospital. My friend had a sweatshirt with the words, "Dr. Jones fixed my bones," and my granddaughter said I should have a shirt with "Dr. Fitz fixed my titts."

They were going to make a uranium mine here [a source of radiation in the town] and build a big hospital, but the people voted against it and now they have no plans for the mine or the hospital. I think it's good not to mine the uranium here. It would hurt the land.

Now, I still skin the small seals and makes the boots. It's good for my arm to clean the skins. I have a good life here. I want to say to everyone who gets the breast cancer to fight for your life. It's hard, so hard.

Interview Analysis

During our interview, Mimi and I sit on the couch of her enclosed porch. The big windows provide an expansive view of her settlement. We sit facing one another and holding hands over the top of the couch. Mimi needs that contact and she holds on tightly. In my role as nurse and provider of care, it is a natural feeling for me to reinforce her courage by holding her hands. Her husband takes part in the interview process. Mimi asks if he could be there because, as she says, "I can't read or write and I need him there for me." She refers to him from time to time and he also replies to questions directed to Mimi. It seems a real partnership, both of them working as one.

During our conversations about Mimi's cancer, her husband becomes very quiet. It is obviously painful for him to remember the events which happened to both of them over 15 years ago. "That is all over now, gone." He then tells me that he wants to forget, but Mimi indicates that it is good to talk it out. She says that her husband never wanted to talk about it, and that talking with me has helped to cleanse herself of all of those memories.

The interview that I have with Mimi and the other informants in Labrador are my first attempted interviews for the process of this work. Now that time has passed and I have been able to reflect on what these women have told me, in some cases, instead of encouraging further reflection on the important events of their lives, perhaps I didn't give them the opportunity.

In Mimi's interview, there were many complex emotions at work. I should have asked her how she felt working as a cleaning girl for the Moravian Missions when other children her age were attending their school. She let me know early on in our relationship that she couldn't read or write.

But it was obvious she was proud of her talent for sewing boots. She was also gratified that she learned late in life to clean skins. After our interview, she lined up five pairs of intricately embroidered seal boots for me to admire. We were able to elaborate on those important accomplishments. When she told me about her brother's death, Mimi began to cry. I asked her about being close to her brother and she told me that she was really close to him (but I didn't give her time to reflect on it long enough). I cried with her.

What did Mimi mean by the statement that she wanted to give up but B_____ (her husband) kept her going? Did she experience feelings of suicide, but wasn't able to say to me that she wanted to kill herself? As I continue to explore women's research techniques, it will be important to remember the true significance of listening. When the formal interview is over, Mimi asks to see herself on the tape. She is elated as we plug the camcorder into her TV. With her whole family gathered about her, I sense their pride. I think that, until this moment, they didn't realize her heroism in undergoing the terrifying experience of breast cancer.

During this time, too, I have the opportunity to speak with Mimi's forty-two-year-old daughter. She tells me that soon after her mother's breast cancer experience, she was terrified for herself. She is afraid to do a breast exam on herself for fear of finding a lump. Until today, those fears are very substantial.

I come away from the interview filled with emotions of my own. I had become very close to Mimi and her husband in two short days. I feel moved to tears by her heroism and her suffering. It is a sad parting. We both promise to continue our relationship. I am part of her life and she is a part of mine. I hold her stories for the world to hear. I am known in her village as "the one who interviewed Mimi."

Labrador, The North Coast, 1993: Ellen's Story

I leave Mimi and B_____'s settlement the next day to catch the Twin Otter to another small village on the north coast. As the plane soars over Mimi's tiny, snow-bound settlement, I wonder if we will meet again. As I strain to look through the condensation on the window, the lilliputian community grows even smaller, finally disappearing from view. It is a long time before I begin to think of meeting the next participant in the project, Ellen.

Ellen: 1993   As in many Inuit settlements, Ellen's community is nestled against the sea in a protected cove. Mimi's husband told me that the ocean water in that cove is so swift that it never freezes. Ellen's house sits quietly on the crest of a glacial moraine overlooking the frozen bay. Two old skid-dos are parked in the front yard.

Ellen's kitchen window, a simple gathering place for her plants, overlooks the small settlement where she lives on the hill. The plant collection gathers dusty sun on a shelf under the smoky window of her kitchen. She cares for them as a mother would care for her children and complains that they look terrible because it is winter. She proudly points out a ragged poinsettia that she rescued from The Northern Store for $3.00. She seems proud of her prowess as a gardener.

Our meeting is informal—two women sharing a morning conversation and stopping for tea. Her table, badly in need of paint, is crowded with used cups, wet tea bags, jelly, and an open loaf of white bread. She shares her tea and bread willingly. Ellen drinks her new herbal teas that I brought from Philadelphia. I drink her Tetley from The Northern Store.

The fire in the wood stove is roaring away in her tiny living room. Inside the little house, it is as hot as a summer day in Philadelphia. I remove sweaters and long underwear and strip down to a T-shirt. Ellen and her husband are bundled up in wool sweaters. On her tiny feet are chartreuse socks which she knitted. They remind me of my greatgrandmother's (Memere) woolen mittens made from scrap yarn. For a fleeting moment, I am taken back to pictures and stories of my childhood and see Memere in her printed house dress and apron sitting in our dusty kitchen window with a half-knitted mitten on her needles, measuring our thumbs. I share these thoughts with Ellen and we both laugh. I remark how wonderful I think her slippers are. Her husband is proud of the crafts that Ellen makes and shows me a set of miniature, beaded moose-hide moccasins that she sells in the craft store. He urges me to accept a set as a gift from Ellen. I am honored that they should want to give me a gift when I have already taken so much from them. I accept graciously. Ellen also weaves grass into wonderfully intricate grass baskets and pots. The sweet smell of grass lingers in my hands.

Ellen begins to speak:

I'm feeling kind of bad today. I was cranky with the nurses on the phone on account of my sore throat, so come on, let's get this over with. We used to live up English River. Oh, it was a hard life but good, too, in a way. I still miss it. I never scraped the skins. As a girl, I would play around, do the dishes, baby sit, things that girls did. My mother went out hunting or fishing to check the traps. We had a little cabin. I would like to turn back the years.

We used to go place to place in the row boat, pick the berries. Go seal hunting in the tent by dog sled. I knows how to use the ulu. I hate making the seal skins, but I can make it. I used to make it for my father. I used to cut and salt the fish—codfish. There's no more codfish here now, but there's lots of seals. My mother died when I was thirteen. My Daddy taught me to do all those things. He taught me to cook, make the seal skin boots. I was close to my daddy. I was the oldest. We never cleaned caribou skins, but we used them [cleaned by someone else] for the tent floors in the hunting camp. We also used them for our mattresses. I went to school up north for three years [Nain]. We used to go up there in September and come home in June. My mother didn't want us to go to school one fall. That was the year she was going to die. She died after she had a baby in the 1918 flu.

The germ arrived aboard the last mail steamer of the 1918 summer. In Hamilton Inlet the boat that transmitted the disease was a motorboat from the supply ship Harmony. Relatives were dead—eaten by the (sled) dogs—nothing left but bones and skulls. There were skulls lying outside of the houses and some bodies. The dogs were really wild. (Saunders, 1981; pp. 30–32)

I don't know what happened here. She had nine babies. Only five of us lived. We used to eat rabbits, deer, partridges, seal, trout, ducks, caribou, wild berries, red berries, black berries, bake apples—everything you see on the land we used to eat it. There was no food in The Northern Stores.

I'm sixty-one. I was eighteen when I had my first child. I breast fed for a little bit until my breasts got sore and then I gave it up. I had five alive with two miscarriages, and two kids died. I would have had nine like my mother. I have three alive, two girls and one son. I was twelve years old when I had my first period. I was forty-eight when I stopped. My grandmother taught me how to be a woman. Her name was Mary. She said that one of these days a man would come along and want me in a different way. I didn't know what she meant by that. My mother died, so I didn't know what to do when I got married. It was the biggest surprise I ever had in my life, I think! It was before my time that people were doing exchange wives and husbands. I hear about it though.

My father and two brothers died of cancer. My father was sixty-six when he died of cancer. My brother was young, in his forties, eh, and the other one had pancreas cancer and he died when he was in his thirties. I don't know about my grandmother and grandfather. All the men had the cancer in my family. I was the only woman, but my sister had cancer in her stomach this summer. She works as a cleaning lady; she's in her forties. But my other sister is healthy. She [the sister who had cancer] had her surgery in Goose Bay. I had my surgery in St. Anthony's and my treatment in St. John's; you go under that thing for three minutes a day for two weeks. I think it's cobalt.

My breast used to be a little bit sore all the time, like a dull ache in there. I didn't even know there was a lump. The doctor found the small little lump and he said to get it out. It was in the hospital in Northwest [River]. [Northwest River is the name of the Hudson's Bay Company post at the mouth of the river. It flows into the western extremity of the Churchill River formerly known as Lake Melville.] They took out the lump and told me that I had to go to St. Anthony's. I was home for a month. I didn't know I had cancer. Then the doctor told me I had cancer, just like that.

I got scared. I was scared that I would die. I was afraid I was going to die. I had a whole lot of kids to look after and my husband to look after and I am going to die. I went in the bathroom and I started to cry. My husband wasn't there and it was really scary. There was a woman from Nain [the northernmost settlement in Labrador settled by Inuit] in the bathroom and she made me feel better. There was no one to help me. I used to hear that if you had cancer you died. I couldn't understand very good what they was going to do with me. I told them to take everything out, right to the bones, I said. I was in St. Anthony's for two weeks and in St. John's for two weeks. I wrote a couple of letters home. My husband can't write, so I never got any letters back. After a while my arm would swell up. The cobalt made me feel like I had a choke feeling. I always wanted to come home. [Barbara Rosenblum also tells of the choking feeling from radiation; see Chapter 3.]

> The side effects of radiation (therapy) are extremely unpleasant, enervating, creeping slowly and catching me unaware. . . . There is a terrible lump in my throat all the time. And it seems that the only way to get rid of it is by swallowing. Yet swallowing is painful and hurts my throat even more. My mouth is always full of saliva. . . . All my throat muscles are in spasm complicating even more what is going on in my esophagus. (Butler & Rosenblum, 1991, p. 41)

Oh, the first time I heard that I had cancer I wanted to jump out of the door there. I was really scared. I thought that my husband wouldn't want me then. That's how I felt. My husband accepted me the way I was and he didn't feel any different. But I was sure that he wouldn't want me. It made me feel as if I was only half a women. I can do anything now. I am stronger.

But every time I have something, like now I have a sore throat since September, or anything going on in my body, I think that its the cancer coming back. I had so many little lumps to deal with. Any little lumps—I want to get this out!

I would like to tell other women to be brave. I thought that people with cancer died right away, see, and I would have to leave my kids behind. I hope my daughters never get it. They know how to look for the lumps. I got three granddaughters. One is at the University, Dalhousie. I am so proud of her.

The nurses of St. John's [Newfoundland] were good. I was able to talk with other women about it in the room. We just talked with all the women. There were no Inuit; that made it worse than ever, you see. It was all *Hablunaks** and I felt that I was alone. The *Hablunaks* were

---

*Hablunaks: An Inuktitut word meaning any non-Inuit; sometimes spelled *Kabluna* or *Kadluna.*

nice, but I wanted to be with my own kind of people to feel safe. You know when you are among your own kind of people, you feel safe.

It feels different with that [other] kind of people. They don't talk the way I talk. *Nakomi* is thank you up here in Inuktitut. If I had to go to St. John's again, I'd like to have someone speak my Inuktitut language and help me feel safe. I would also like to eat my own kind of foods in the hospital. You can't get them in a snare. Just go to the store and get it. It makes you lazy. Me and my brother used to go to the same old tree to get the partridges. Not take too many, just enough for one day and go back the next day. They would always be there.

Every year I go for a check up. I go to St. Anthony, Newfoundland, in April every year. The doctor was the one who made me feel better. He talked to me real nice like a good doctor. He didn't brush me off.

I prayed a lot. I'm Anglican, not Moravian. And even sometimes I don't think He hears me. When we was children, my mother gave us "Indian teas" for sore throat [Ledum or Labrador tea]. I still takes it if I can finds it.

Even going to Goose Bay is better than going to St. Anthony for check up. And come back the next day [from Goose Bay] and you go out there [to St. Anthony's] and wait and wait. The mission plane takes me.

I wish that there was someone to talk to breast cancer women in their own language and have a women's group. If we had a women's group here, it would be better than just gossiping all day. I wish they had a mammography in Goose Bay for check up rather than going to St. Anthony. [Goose Bay is an hour by plane from Ellen's settlement. Women could have their mammogram early in the morning and go home the same day. When they go to St. Anthony, it is at least a three-day trip with two plane changes.]

I'm glad that you came to visit me today. I feel better now that you came to see me. I was going to say that I was going away so that I wouldn't have to see you, but I'm glad I saw you. I'm glad to help other women.

Interview Analysis

Ellen's husband is afflicted with cardiac problems. She "forbids" him to go alone out into the woods because she is fearful that he will die out there. The situation forces them to depend on their oldest son to gather firewood from the forest. Her husband, a former hunter, sits passively through some of the interview and seems lost for the first time in his life. She also told me that she felt sick on the day of the interview and seems cross or angry when I call. Before we begin the interview, I give her some honey in warm water and tea. It makes an improvement in her sore throat. She is upset because she wants me to speak with her in Inuktitut. I tell her that I am learning the language and speak all the words I know. We laugh at my feeble attempts, and the bond between us is made. She tells me, "We think the Hablunaks are smart when they can speak our language."

Because I make an attempt to speak Ellen's language, she accepts me in spite of my language limitations. Ellen is bilingual, fluent in English as well as Inuktitut. One of Ellen's major concerns, and it is a valid one, is that nurses and doctors are unable to communicate in Inuktitut to the patients. In the Northwest Territories, the hospital in Iqaluit has Inuit translators for the patients. Ellen is proud of her Inuk heritage. Her language and customs are very important to her. She tells me about her experience in going to school for four years in Northwest River where she "went through hell if I spoke my own language." She didn't teach her kids the language because of what she went through at school. "I'm sorry now that they never learned," she concludes.

Ellen's greatest fear is cancer recurrence. She is angry and upset at the prospect. She is also upset over her health care providers' inabilities to speak to her in Inuktitut. It is frightening for her to think about going through surgery again. Cancer recurrence is a fear among all breast cancer survivors.

Labrador, Goose Bay—Happy Valley, 1994

Journal 12/31/93 It is New Year's Eve in Goose Bay and darkness falls at 4:00 P.M. When we land from Rigolet, the airport is shrouded in gloomy light and snow is falling. It is difficult to see the runway. The plane lands suddenly. Before going to the bed and breakfast, I stop at the only restaurant open, The Hong Kong. I ordered curried chicken, but when it arrives I am unable to eat. It reminds me of vomited crud. I think of my Mom vomiting at home. I call her in the morning to wish her a Happy New Year's Day. It is 8:00 A.M. in Boston and she can't figure out who I am. It sounds as if she has been awake all night. Her speech is slurred. I have spent the last ten days with Inuit women, heroes who have survived breast cancer, their families and their love intact. I want my mother to be a hero. It hurts to have her in denial with a bottle of Seagram's. I want her to know that I am safe. I want to share the ten days of interviews with her. Conversation is impossible. "I'll be fine. I'll be fine. Nothing is wrong with me," she repeats. I think that her cancer has invaded her bones at last. Dad says that she wants to die, that she has nothing to live for. She really needs to see the doctor. She needs morphine and a hospital. I hang up the phone, my heart is heavy. I feel alone, a failure, and though I should cry, I don't.

New Year's Day in Labrador! I have appointments to interview three other women who live in the Goose Bay–Happy Valley area. But it is New Year's Day and I don't schedule an interview because I feel that it would be intrusive. I take the car and drive down to the Northwest River section. On the way, I look in vain for caribou or other signs of wildlife, but this is the city, and animals have been driven off. The sun is brilliant, the road slick, and snowmobiles are everywhere. There are no restaurants open in all of Goose Bay.

Goose Bay, 1994: Lilly

Lilly is from north of Labrador and is a relative to one of the women with whom I have spoken while I was in the North. She lives alone on the outskirts of Goose Bay, but wants very much to move with her son back to the North Coast. Her cozy house is modest, clean, and decorated with a large Christmas tree. The television is the focus of her living room. She is dressed in a white Western-cowboy style fringed shirt, wears rhinestone dangling earrings and a bracelet, and greets me smiling broadly.

Lilly begins to speak:

> I was going to a doctor for a year. And I had no blood test, no X-ray for a year. I was going every three months. Then that doctor went away and I phoned up to the hospital. I was takin' a bath and I felt the lump right there in my breast. So I went up to see the doctor and he gave me a blood test. He said that there is something eating the salt from your blood. You need to take another test. After two weeks I went back again to another doctor but he wouldn't see me. So I visited my son and I come back and saw Dr. Tate. "You might lose your breast, you have cancer.

Mrs. you have cancer and there is nothing I can do for you," he said. I was steaming. He came back and referred me to "a good friend over at the health center; I am going to send you over there."

The cancer had gone under my arm. I didn't know what breast cancer was, never had a thought of it. My husband was still alive. [When the surgery was over] someone whispered in my ear, "It was a successful operation." I took cobalt treatment for nine days. I was nine days in the health science [department]. We did the exercise "Hoist the Flag." I went to the Orange Home in St. John's. The cobalt made me sick. We was all sat around the table. "Mrs. You have to eat," the doctor said.

I was born up north in Aillik Cape. The Norwegians came over and they jumped ship and they married the native women.

I still have my Moravian church hat.

All the girls have new Church caps (for Easter), a custom from the old Moravian Church. Unmarried sisters have pink ribbons, married sisters blue and widows white, a huge bow under their chin. The caps are crocheted in white wool or made of white lace." (Saunders (Ed.) Steadman, 1993; p. 14)

My husband had the cancer [prostate cancer]. He lived eight years. Mine was the 15th of September, 1983. My Mom's mother died of cancer of the skin. My sister had cancer of the blood, leukemia.

I knew Elizabeth Goudie. [Elizabeth Goudie is Labrador's most famous woman. She wrote a book on life in Labrador in the late 1800s.] She lived just up the road from me near the Hudson Bay Store. My husband was a trapper and a hunter. He hunted seals, birds, foxes, caribou. I made my husband's boots. He was from the north, Jim A's brother, Edward. [Jim A is Mimi's brother-in-law.] His mother taught me to make the boots. She would yell at me if they weren't right. I used the sinew from the back of the caribou. You have to cut the back of the caribou right down the back and that makes good meat cakes. And you dry it and that makes good sinew. My grandmother taught us the string games and the button games on a string.

I grew up in Aillik Cape. But we used to go around all over in the boat with my Dad between Nain and Postville. Have you been way North? You can see all the big icebergs and everything. I was the oldest: me and my brother Johnny. We used to row around in the boat, with Dad fishing. We used to catch codfish just as long as this table here.

When I was first married, me and my husband used to row around in the boat, fishing. One time we was way down the shoal, fishing, and Dad was fishing and I was fishing and my brother Johnny was fishing, and Dad says, "I got something, a shark or something." And he hauls out and I looked and there was white comin' up, and I said, "That's an old man shark," and Dad says, "Oh no that's a young lassie." He said, "You hold on to the old jigger," like this and shook it in the water and I was shivverin' like that, scared, but I kept holding on to the jigger and my dad shot the shark. And we hauls it aboard. It was an old sick one and we give it to the dogs. Another thing, we used to be way down the shoals and dad sees a grampus or a jumper. Some people call jumpers and them that's all whales, but that's not [correct]; its jumpers, there's porpoises and whales. We chased it in the bottom of the boat and I was hidin' inside the bottom of the boat. Dad says, "You foolish little thing." Today I am still afraid in the boat. Another time we went down fishin' again and we caught a big shark. We was fishin' by a sea island, Rigid Island, and we went into a little cove. And I was up in the "stem" [stern] and the rudder broke and we went smack into the cliff. The boat smashed and all the stuff went down. We rowed to another boat, they rescued us. Another time I was in a boat that caught fire—no dory or nothing. It was a foolish way it happened. Sam [my brother] lit a cigarette off the engine. And Dad says, "Take off your clothes," and we smashed the fire out with our coats. That's why I am afraid in a boat. I won't go down to St. John's in the boat.

I went to school three months to the Moravian School. I runned away one time. I was stayin' with my grandmother. I was six years old. Sarah Oku's Mom was stayin' over in Aillik. I went over to my Aunt Mary's house. My Mom come to get me. I can read and write my name. We had hard books in those days. The Moravians spoke German in those days. My Dad could talk Inuktitut, but my Mom can't. He was ninety-nine years old when he died. When he died he sat up like he was at the table eatin' dinner. My mom lived to be eighty-four. She died of diabetes. We used to eat all our fresh meat from the land. My grandmother took us berry pickin'. We had partridge berries, but not crow berries [Empetrum nigrum], they's poison, we used to eat bake apples [called Salmon Berries in Alaska and Cloud Berries in The Northwest Territories: Rubus chamaemorus].

I had only one son, but I didn't breast feed him. I was around thirty when he was born. I was twelve years old when I had my first period. I finished at fifty-five. I had cancer twice. I had cancer of the cervix. But

I never had no treatment for that. I went through the change of life. I had a doctor's book and I was always readin' this doctor's book and I come across that. If you're up in your fifties and you was 'ministratin' and it came out a dark color it could be cancer. So I was workin' in the hotel up there so I said to the girl, "I'm going to see the doctor, I'm ministratin." And the young doctor said to come up Monday mornin' and we'll give you a D&C. So he said you got to go to St. Anthony to have everything taken out. That was 1970. I didn't know anything about that going under the knife. In 1983 I had my breast off. After I had my breast cancer, I couldn't work like I did before.

My Mom was the one who told me about being a woman and to stay away from the boys, like that you know. She told me I was a woman now and not to play with the boys in the wrong way. She said I might have children. The first boyfriend I had—when I kissed him I thought I was pregnant. They was strict in them days. My dresses had to be right down there [to below the knee]. If my dress was too short, my dad would say to my Mom, "Make that old maid's dress a little longer. That dress is too short." And we had to scrub the hard wood floors with the brush, and if it wasn't right we would have to do it over again. I got lots of brothers: fourteen children, seven boys and seven girls. They is all younger than me. My sister Nancy died of cancer of the blood. And I had a sister died in Newfoundland. She died of TB; Jane was her name.

My husband was a quiet man and he was OK with my breast cancer and he was OK with himself because you see he had his cancer too [of the prostate]. [Lilly is talking about having sexual relations with her husband. Her husband was impotent because of his prostate cancer. Because he himself was sick, he didn't feel any differently about Lilly because of her breast cancer.]

When you lose a breast, you'll never know, only the person what has it done can know. I didn't feel too good when I left the hospital. I went in there into my room at the Orange Home and put my suitcase down and sat down on the bed; and something came over me and I wanted to tear the curtains down and tear the bed and the room apart. You know who I thought about? Terry Fox—and I put my hand up like that and I said I was going to be like Terry Fox. [Terry Fox was a young Canadian athlete who lost a leg to cancer. In order to create an awareness of cancer and to raise money for cancer research in Canada, Terry Fox began a run across Canada. Halfway through his run, he died of cancer.]

When I go to buy dresses at first, I couldn't buy them because my breast was gone. I had a lot of lonely days and nights.

I want to tell other women to keep their courage up if they have anything done like that. And go and see a doctor right away if they have a lump anywhere.

If I had told the doctor that I had the lump it would have been better. I want my granddaughters to have a good life, to keep checking. There was another Eskimo woman when I was growing up and she had a big hole in her breast all red and she died. I often think about her.

I keep my spirits up and that helped me. I prayed a lot too. And I prayed with another Salvation Army woman in the Orange Home and she helped me. People should take care of themselves right from their being young.

Interview Analysis

Cold, wet snow from the Maritimes blows against the windows of Lilly's house. It blankets flowers and rattles the panes of glass. Inside, Lilly treats me warmly, like family. We sit at her kitchen table like grandmother and granddaughter having a serious chat. She is generous and is lonely for company. After the interview, we share her bulging family album. It is a special moment to glimpse these frozen vignettes of her personal life. "This is a picture of me when I used to clean house for the Americans on the base," she says. "Here is my weddin' picture." Lilly is a mirthful, jovial woman, as ponderous as she is generous. Nevertheless, anger and fear surface when telling stories of how she had to deal with unknowns—something, she tells me, that she doesn't think about anymore. Because of her husband's "prostrate" cancer, they didn't have any sex life by the time Lilly had her breast cancer. It seems as though he was supportive as much as he could be. Surviving breast cancer is a victory. Lilly was able to overcome her own fears by thinking of Terry Fox's life ending so young from cancer. As she reminisced about stories of her youth and life on the North Coast, I detected a yearning to return to a passionate life with friends that she once knew.

Labrador, Goose Bay—Happy Valley, 1994: Sally

I travel to Goose Bay on January 2nd to meet with the youngest of the informants in Labrador. Her house, a modern duplex near the center of Goose Bay, is located on a mundane suburban street in North America. I mentally note that her generation is far from the trapper's life of her grand-fathers and mothers. Sally welcomes me warmly and tells me that she is nervous. We talk about what is causing her nervousness. For a few min-utes, we sit at her dining room table and gossip over coffee. I comment on her magnificent Christmas tree and decorations. I have brought a gift for her grandson. Although he has many toys, Sally and I watch him open this new one and play with it. He is amused for the moment, but soon is cling-ing to Sally's side seeking attention. Sally seems more at ease. People here are hungry for news from the North Coast and I tell her news from Rigolet and Makkovik. She is humble, explaining, "I'm only one of the locals." Sally and her husband are renovating their house and she apologizes for the clutter on the porch. Her Inuit heritage comes from her grandfather who lived around Mud Lake, where she grew up.

We talk about the caribou herd and hunting on the North Coast. She feels that the caribou are contaminated somehow and are causing cancer in the population, noting that even young girls are getting cancer. "I think it's from eating wild meat," she observes. Her thoughts concerning the caribou are interesting. (See Appendix A for more information about this.)

Dominating the dining room is a glass credenza holding her magnifi-cent porcelain doll collection. She tells me that she loves kids and I wonder if the dolls are a substitute for the children. She is forty-seven-years-old, the caregiver for her three-year-old grandson, and teaches at the recreation center.

Sally begins telling her story:

Life in Goose Bay was a lot more fun then than it is now, I'll tell you. Even with this cold weather, we would dress up and go out. We used to come over to Goose Bay from Mud Lake on the dog sled. My father worked for the Americans at the base.

Ownership of Labrador has bounced back and forth between the French and the British since 1500. A Privy Council* decision in 1927 awarded Labrador to Newfoundland and established the present boundary between Quebec and Labrador. But Quebec has

---

*Privy Council: A council of British sovereigns that until the 17th century was the supreme legis-tative body. The Privy Council consists of cabinet ministers ex officio and others with membership for life. It acts as a judicial committee.

never accepted the boundary decision; its official maps show
Labrador as part of Quebec territory. Labrador and Newfoundland
joined Canada in 1949. (Petro-Canada, 1978, p. 2)

He took the dog team over. We used to ride in the *komatik*. I never drove
the team, but I did take out the lead dog. I remember smoking in the
woods when I was a kid. We played the cat's cradle and the button-on-
the string game [buzzer]. We had toys for Christmas and we had a bike
among the four of us when we was growing up.

The population of Northwest River was fifty or sixty people, but we
called them all aunties and uncles to show respect. When I got to be
thirteen I used to help clean the fish. I was a tom boy. I have two older
sisters and two younger brothers. I'm differn't from the rest of them.
I'm more out-spoken than they are. When I had breast cancer I still
said that I wasn't sick. That was four years ago. It might have been in
1988.

I used to clean and skin rabbits and fish, but not seals. My mom used
to make seal boots, but she never taught us how to do it. She didn't have
time, I guess. She didn't bother teaching us because she had too much
time with the youngsters, I 'spose. She had a baby every three years.
Sometimes I regrets not learnin' how to sew or knit; I can still pick it
up, though. If I had anything that needs sewin', or knittin' I bring it to
her. She never really taught us anythin' by sittin' down and teachin' you,
but we learned by watching.

I went to school in Mud Lake until I was fifteen years old, but then
my Dad and grandfather got sick with T.B., and of course they had to go
off to St. Anthony. So I was taken out of school to look after the younger
children—I never finished school. I went to 8th grade. Mom had to go
to work and she left me home with the kids. My younger sisters were
still in school.

Mud Lake, with a population of 90, was settled by fishermen more
than 150 years ago. The first large-scale sawmilling operation was
established there in 1900. After the mill closed in 1915, the community once more became a village of trappers and fishermen.
(Petro-Canada, 1978, p. 8)

Me and my friends talk about it [our food] sometime every once in a
while and, you know, we can't remember havin' a chicken or a roast in

the house. We used to eat country food, caribou, fish, ducks, lynx or mountain cat, even bear meat. I suppose we had turkey at Christmas time though.

I was twenty-six when I had my first child. I was single, but it was the feller I married to have my children. I didn't breast feed. I guess it restricts you. So many people that's breast feeding tell me that you waste your time. You don't have time for yourselves. I had a friend in Yarmouth and she [her daughter] still takes the breast at three years old. I was feeding mine caribou soup when they was two weeks old.

I was fourteen or fifteen when I had my first period. There was a minister who had a bible school in the summer and it was the last day and we had a big picnic and of course I got sick. I knew what was going on in one sense and then again I didn't. Mom happened to be home, thank goodness, and I had to go to bed and I can remember it was sore, sore, sore. Yep, I must have been fourteen or fifteen. I learned how to be woman, that it just come natural. Mom never spoke about anythin'; I just watched because there was no televisions or nothin' in them days to teach you anything. My sisters were ashamed. They said, "Tsk tsk," if I spoke about anything. One of my sisters is fifty. She never will be married. She lives with a man.

She has one child about thirty-two, and another about seven years old, but she never got married. But the boy that she's was livin' with ended up in the hospital with bleeding ulcers. He had an operation and somethin' went wrong about fifteen years ago and he died and now she's livin' with another man. I never had any sisters die of breast cancer, but I had an aunt who died last year of cancer, stomach cancer. She never smoked or drank.

I still have my period. My menopause is cookin' though. I have three kids—a daughter and two sons.

My Daddy died of havin' a stroke. My Mom's still alive and she had a stroke. She is in the home. She knows people, but can't speak. She is seventy-three. She looks young. My kids all live at home. My daughter will be twenty or twenty-one. My other son is twenty-three. No jobs to kick them out. They got their trade though. One is a mechanic and one in auto body. If there was work, they would leave Labrador, but you have to have money to do that. Everyone wants experienced people. If you don't have experience, they won't hire you.

My aunt died of stomach cancer at sixty. I don't have check-ups anymore [for breast cancer]. The doctor told me I didn't need any. But, if I go on holiday, I go to St. Anthony for the mammogram, but it makes me so sore. I don't like it. I found the lump in my breast myself. I was just getting ready for bed and at the same time I was having problems with my stomach. I went back and forth to the doctor and they didn't really know. It was just right there getting red and hard and, I guess, within a week's [time after an] appointment I just was going to bed one night and I put my hand up [to my breast] like that and I found it. My husband was workin' and it kind of scared me. The first thing that struck my mind was cancer. When the doctor told me [that it was cancer of the breast], it didn't bother me. I thought that it [the breast] could come off. That's all I thought of. Still didn't strike me that it could go farther.

I let everyone else worry about it. I went to St. John's. I had my gall bladder removed four years before and the same Dr. Tarva did it. I didn't need any treatment or anything for it. It wasn't in the node, but it was there a long time. I was in five days and the day I got out, I went in the helicopter to my husband's fish camp at Ann Marie Lake.

After we made love for the first time, I guess my husband had some feelings there but it seemed OK. Even now I don't like to look at it because of one side gone, you know. Cuz its ugly. I wouldn't have reconstruction, even if that were an option for me.

I would like to see that my daughter gets more check-ups but she won't. She is the same as my sister. But I want them to do it. You have to go to St. John's to have a mammogram, but my husband has insurance for me to go and have it. I would like to see a mammogram in Goose Bay. There was a telethon a few months ago for some other machine, so they could get another one. There's a lot of people in Goose Bay comin' down with cancer, so we need to get the mammogram here soon.

I never really spoke about my cancer with anyone. My husband was afraid. I'd go down to my mother's a lot for some reason. The doctor told me I had cancer and I, all I thought of was, well, it can come off. I don't let things bother me. My husband went with me to St. John's. I'm not that religious, but I believe in god. But it's not going to make you live any longer.

If any woman finds a lump, go and have it checked out right away. Don't leave it too long. My husband made me go right away. It seems that a lot of people around here are getting cancer these days. I just heard of another young girl who had cancer of the stomach. Some people think that it's from eating wild meat, but not everyone eats wild meat.

It is important to go and get checked out. Some women won't do it. There was a woman who had a lump under her arm and she didn't get it checked and died of breast cancer.

Interview Analysis

Developed in Sally's early youth, there seems to be a sense of independence that stabilizes the calm when turmoil hits. Sally is tough in her approach to life and in dealing with her cancer, but a hint of fatalism shadows her attitude about breast cancer. "I'll let others worry about it," she says.

Sally never went into detail about her feelings when she made love for the first time after her breast was removed. Even now she doesn't like to look at her scar "cuz its ugly." Although I may look for fear in her, because of Sally's lifestyle, she assumes a tenacious veneer. It was good to talk with Sally; I believe she felt the same in my regard, too. "I never really talked with anyone about my cancer before," she admitted. I should have asked how it felt to be taken out of school to care for her younger siblings, but I know she would have been resigned to that as she is to her cancer. She is so like the women of the North, thinking of others before self, concerned about the economy, her family, the lack of work in a cash economy.

Labrador, 1994: Jean

Jean's story cannot be told. Although agreeing to participate in the interviews when I called her from Philadelphia, Jean's son committed suicide and was buried on Christmas Eve. I heard about her awful tragedy when I was on the North Coast. When I arrived in Goose Bay after interviewing on the North Coast, I called Jean to let her know how sorry I was about her son. She was polite and guarded with her emotions. Through the sound of her voice, I could hear her distress and sadness. When I suggested that she not participate, she seemed relieved. Women in Labrador are givers and, even in her pain, I feel Jean would have participated. I didn't want to intrude on her life five days after the funeral. Jean said that I could send her the questions, which I did. But when I called her two months later, she told me that she still couldn't think. I gave her my phone number and asked her to call me collect if ever I could help her, but I know she won't call. She won't want to be a "bother."

SUMMARY: REFLECTION ON PERSONS, PLACES, AND PROCESS

Up and down Labrador's North Coast, we gathered to tell our stories around warm cups of coffee or tea set on kitchen tables. For the first time, I realize the significance of the kitchen table as a vehicle of communication for women. Their stories are fresh. They swirl around my imagination like falling snow, like pieces in a puzzle.

By participating in the interview process itself, the women in the study gained a sense of empowerment and realized the need for breast cancer screening closer to home. In fact, one of the women in Goose Bay–Happy Valley told me, "Some people here in town had a big telethon for a machine to measure cancer; I suppose that we could to the same for a mammography." Because of a blizzard, there is a plane delay in Montreal. I call my Mom and there is a long time to talk. She sounds happier. Her ear is better and the pain in her back is diminished. I ask her when she'll be seeing the doctor. "I'm fine," she answers.

Journal Entry: 1/2/94 The holidays pass quickly. I am excited about the work in Labrador. By scheduling only one interview a day, I have time to process the words of the stories and to reflect on what the informants have told me. I have gained much. It has been exciting to listen to stories, to meet survivors living in the North, and to experience their winter environment.

I have also encountered their strength, their laughter, their joy. I am stronger as a result. The harsh Labrador land matches the strength of her women. They are both part of me now and I welcome their gifts. Back in the Philadelphia suburbs, a long way from the North Coast, I sit at my own kitchen table, alone, cradling a cup of gourmet coffee and pondering what to do as the "Keeper" of the stories.

Journal Entry: 4/13/94 My mother's cancer seems to be in remission, and for the moment, she is focusing on my father's surgery for prostate cancer instead of her own problems. She often obliterates her memory with drink, but not so acutely as last winter. I plan my phone calls carefully, so that she will be clear-headed when I call.

Journal Entry: 6/27/93 On the Road to Denver and to Anchorage Kansas gold spreads out in all directions. Outcrops of limestone, evidence of ancient seas, are favorite haunts for Red Tail Hawks and turkey vultures. The wind blows over waving fields of golden wheat and oats. Here and there sunflowers nod along the highway, following the circle of the sun. I am like the sunflowers following my own sun circle.

Because of a previous commitment to work in Alaska as a research assistant with a team from the University of Colorado for the summer, I leave from Denver to interview the women in Anchorage. I am at the bifurcation of my life, taking a path that is unknown and leaving a life that has been familiar for many years. When I return from Anchorage this year, I'll settle in Montana. This is my rite of passage from the old to the new and I welcome it.

I am my own company. My thoughts are random and run freely inside my head as the music from the car radio brings me home to Philadelphia. I wonder why I am doing this—grabbing at life with both hands—wanting to have all experiences before death gives me back to the Dancing Lights. Life is precious. [The Inuit believed that when death called a member of their clan, they went to the Northern Lights, which they called The Dancing Lights.]

Journal Entry: 7/5/94 Anchorage: 1995 Anchorage, a bustling city of over a quarter million, sprawls over the mountainsides and valley of the Chugach Range. The women in Anchorage are excited and eager to be interviewed. They are younger, more sophisticated than the other women, urbanized, well educated, and some work outside the home. Some are a generation younger than the women in Labrador. Most have researched their treatment options. For others, their options have been exhausted. Many are in their early forties or middle fifties. I contact them by phone. They all want to help other native women and to have their voices heard.

Their generosity to the project and to one another demonstrates to me that the Inuit and native sharing process continue to be culturally alive and that women continue to give to other women. Is this what makes them native or Inuit—the sharing?

Journal Entry: 7/13/94   The informants for Alaska Voices have been contacted. They are excited to tell their story to someone who will really listen. Their voices are angry voices, angrier than the women in Labrador, angry that in many cases their diagnosis was not detected earlier, especially for those living in remote villages. Because of the hiatus in treatment, some of the women are now in stage three with metastasis.

Stories from Alaska: Summer 1994

Joan: 1994

Joan is a modern Inupiat woman in her mid-forties who, before her breast cancer diagnosis, worked for the government. Her split-level home is beautifully furnished with comfortable, expensive furniture and collections of figurines and other bric-a-brac of one sort or another. Her six-year-old son and her husband are the center of her universe which is reflected in her eyes when she talks about them.

Joan had been cancer-free for over ten years and recently was diagnosed with cancer in her second breast with twenty-seven nodes positive. In spite of her guarded prognosis, Joan is optimistic, cheerful, and in love with life. Next summer, she plans to plant flowers in her yard. She had just returned from Seattle where she was one of the first Alaska natives to undergo an experimental treatment in removing bone marrow stem cells and returning them to the body. She is grateful to have been able to participate in this still very experimental procedure. [Joan died in February, 6 months after our interview, her summer flower garden left barren.]

Joan's Story

I'm half Eskimo, and my Mom is from the Malamute tribe. I was born in Omaha, Nebraska. My mother met my father on an air base in Nome and they moved to Nebraska. I have brother who was born in Nome and there is less than a year's difference between us. I have another brother who was born in Anchorage. I lived in Nebraska until I was about nine years old. Then my parents got divorced and we moved back to Anchorage. My life was pretty normal on the air force base. I was a tomboy with my two brothers. My mom got westernized down there, but she does sew with skins and furs. She is allergic to fur. She makes tall *mukluks* [Kamiks]. I wasn't interested in learning to sew, but I took sewing lessons, but its been a year since I've sewn. I learned about sex from kids in school and a little from my mom. She is still traditional; it's too taboo to go into the nitty gritty about sex. I was about twelve or thirteen when I had my first period. Almost all of my school years have been in Anchorage. I'm not into seal oil or *muktuk*, but my mom is. She remarried and there are four more of us from my mom's second marriage who all eat Eskimo food. The smell of Eskimo food doesn't agree with me.

The first time I got married I was 19 and had my first child when I was 20. I also have a grandchild now and there is a year-and-a-half difference between my son and my grandson. They chase each other around. It feels kind of weird. I didn't breast feed my kids. I was too uncomfortable with it the first time and when Lee was born in between my two breast cancers, I already had a mastectomy, so I was leery about it. I am the second oldest and no other kids have cancers. My mother is still alive and my father lives in Nebraska. I remember going to my grandmother's funeral [father's side] and she died of cancer, but I don't know what kind.

I was separated from my first husband [he left soon after her first mastectomy] and was covered by his insurance. I was real faithful about going every year and keeping up with gynecological [exams]. I was taking a shower and was scrubbing my breast and found the lump, so I called my doctor right away. The doctor didn't like the look of it, and sent me to a surgeon who did a biopsy. It took a week for the test to come back. I had a gut feeling that it was cancer all along. I have fibrocystic disease. I had a modified mastectomy and the cancer had spread to the first lymph node. I had the surgery downtown and when my divorce became final I went to the native hospital and Claudette was my chemo nurse. I had a terrible time and my veins collapsed. I had to soak in hot water so the veins would pop up. I took three different medicines, and lost my hair. It was a long time before I could even think IV [intravenous]—it nauseated me. I couldn't take pot because I worked for the government. This time I've been really faithful; I had my mammogram in June or July and it was almost ten years to the month [of my last mastectomy]. Because of the fibrocystic it [the breast] was always so tender, but this time I couldn't even touch it. On my regular gyn exam, while the doctor was treating me for pre-menopause, I mentioned that my breast was really tender. So she started feeling around on it and found the lump. She sent me right away down the hall. They decided they would do surgery because they could feel the lymph nodes. It was the day before Thanksgiving and the day after [Thanksgiving] I had the biopsy.

I was operated on the next week. My husband was with me when they told me. I had a mammogram in June or July and they didn't pick it up. I had big breasts anyway, size D, so it was torture to squeeze it under the plate. My breast had only been tender for a couple of months. This cancer was much faster growing and it wasn't a recurrence from the first one. It was a new cancer. How many women can say they had breast cancer twice? They say one in nine women gets it, so I feel that I took someone else's breast cancer.

I was going to have chemo for five and a half months, but they stopped it and I had to go to Seattle to the Fred Hutchenson Cancer Research Center where I had stem-cell infusion. I was part of a study where some of the group had bone marrow transplants and some had stem-cell infusion. I had to have this so I could survive. This way I have a better chance and they are very optimistic. I didn't have any insurance because no one would insure me. It was $150,000 for the treatment. I went down with another girl from Anchorage. We are the only Native Alaskan people who have had it. [The Indian Health Service paid the bill for Joan's treatment.] At the hospital in Seattle where they give the stem-cell infusion treatment you have to have a caregiver, so my sister went with me. She is 31. Her work allowed her to go with me; we were there for six and a half weeks. All of the medicine and the chemo made me very nauseous. I had a Hickman line on the chest where they could draw blood and give the stem-cell infusion and the chemo with it. It was a lot better than getting poked every day. One pill was ten dollars! I had CAT scans and bone scans. The cost of the pills is so much. I had headaches and lower back pains for three days. The stem cells are separated by a machine and are removed from the blood and the blood is returned to the body. I had a bone marrow aspiration and a consultation. It was awful. They collect the stem cells for three days. They must use a preservative and when they come back in [via intravenous], they smell like creamed corn. The computer on the hydration bag is set for three to twelve hours a day. My sister took classes to learn how to use the computer to do this. She changed my dressing every day. The doctor was pleased with my results, but I did get an infection. They put me on antibiotics right away and more hydration. My sister was my caregiver and took me to the doctor appointments; she fed me; made me take my pills; she was a blessing. My husband came down when I started my chemo and he was very supportive. I couldn't ask for a more loving husband. This is the second time for him [going through breast cancer with her].

To other women I would say: Learn to do your own breast exam; ask questions; keep up with the readings; especially if you have had someone in your family with breast cancer. They are coming out with all sorts of new treatments. There is a new technique for mammogram as well. I wish they had that for me. For husbands, try to be understanding. It is more traumatic for the family. It is emotional for the family; it is really hard. Help to cook and clean. I don't know how my husband can put up with it. I try to keep a positive attitude and down the road, day to day, I ask myself, "Will I be here?" You need a positive attitude—it's that or die. Talk to the doctors, nurses, minister, or friends—you can't keep problems bottled up. After my first cancer, I went to the psychiatrist because I thought that something was wrong, I was too positive. With this cancer, it's a little harder [emotionally] and it is an extreme cancer. A three-year outlook is good for this kind of cancer. A five-year is better, but the percentages get less. With the first cancer I lasted ten years and had a child in between! I had a child five years ago exactly to the month of my first mastectomy and he is so precious! I am not an extremely religious person, but I feel that this is just a test of my faith.

As far as dietary changes, I have tried to cut down on red meat. I am happy the way things went, and I am so happy to be home. My greatest fear is that I won't be around for my son when he grows up and for my grandson, and that my husband and I won't grow old together. [Joan began to cry at this point and we stopped for a few minutes.] But I have a good attitude and I am hoping for the best. Making love is coming back. You kind of lose your desire after a while. It is hard on B_____. We love each other, to feel and touch, but my body has been through a lot, and I am self-conscious about my body and about losing my breast. Losing my breast the first time didn't bother my husband at all. He said, "They took my favorite one." It [sex drive] is gradually coming back; as my body gains in strength, it will come back.

[I offer to stay with her son if she and her husband want to engage in a little romantic afternoon. She laughs, and although both of them are pleased with the offer, she isn't ready.]

It is so important to have the support of family and friends. I am looking forward to retirement and being a housewife. It is important to do what you want to do and to take time to love your family and friends and spouse. Do it now so because it can be taken away so quickly. I am going to get involved in my son's school. I am going to enjoy life.

Interview Analysis

Joan praised her doctors who were good and genuinely concerned about her condition. She never felt like killing herself, because of the love she feels for her family. She could never deprive them of that love. However, she did state that, when going through treatment, "You want to get well or quietly fade away." She treasures every minute of her life and is planning for her future. She talked about the bald women in the Seattle hospital, the people from all over the world who came to the treatment center, and the family feeling there, with everyone caring for one another. Jokingly, she pulled off her wig to show me how she looks without her hair. "I bet you'd like to get that on videotape," she said laughing. Joan feels so thankful for the opportunity to have the stem-cell treatment. She is so thankful that the treatment has given her an extension of the quality of her life. The love she feels radiates out to all who come in contact with her. From the sound of her voice and her husband's tenderness, her love life will be returning soon. Yet it still seemed that Joan was unable to articulate more of her feelings of self-consciousness without her breasts.

Joan is proud of her heritage. After our lengthy interview, she was eager to display intricate ivory and wooden carvings of bears, seals, and other animals designed by her brother. Although seemingly hidden behind a facade of acculturation, she thinks about the traditional, cultural crafts of the Inupiat-Malamutes and wonders if it can be useful for her healing.

Maxine: 1994

Maxine is the name chosen for her by her mother at birth. Her name was changed, but for this project, Maxine preferred this name for herself to maintain her family's confidentiality. Choosing to interview at Carr's supermarket in Anchorage rather than in the privacy of her home, we arranged to meet in the coffee shop. "You'll know me," she said over the phone. "I'll be wearing a bright blouse and a hat." She told me that she had three wigs, but doesn't want to "show them off." As I sat waiting in the coffee shop trying to ignore the din made by traffic, the blaring intercom, and the numbers of curious onlookers, I wondered how we would have any privacy. Outside, there was a public picnic area; it wasn't ideal, but it afforded more privacy. Then I saw Maxine. I can never forget how she looked that day. She had a radiance about her—whether from love or joy, I'll never know. She was beaming her broad smile and wearing a wonderful brown, leather cap. Circling her neck was an exquisite beaded necklace with matching earrings in her pierced ears. I knew her at once; we rushed over and celebrated our meeting with a long hug. She felt warm, comfortable. We both felt at ease. I was meeting a long lost friend. She had just returned from the lower forty-eight where her eldest son graduated from law school. She was radiant with pride! Maxine works as a social worker with troubled youth encouraging them to stay in school. She is forty-eight-years-old. Again, I am cognizant that we are two women sitting at a table.

Maxine's Story

I was born in Wainwright, Alaska, one hundred miles west of Barrow at the top of the world. It was a simple life. We didn't have conveniences or stores like we do now. Everybody was friendly, busy making a living. My mother and my dad were childhood sweethearts. They went to school together. As my mom got older, my grandfather sent my mom and her sister to California for training, so they would be of some help to the village. My mom became a teacher and my aunt came back an RN. My grandfather was Commissioner of Alaska and came from Ireland. He was a sailor and came to Alaska via San Francisco. He settled in Wainwright and was a whaler and trader. One of my earliest memories was when I was just three years old and my aunt took me to grandma's sod house with a ceiling light [hole to the sky]. I remember coming in there and I was scared. There were no windows. I cried and cried and they took me out. People still lived in sod houses then, about twenty years ago.

There are two or three hundred people now [in Wainwright]. I helped my mother sew jackets for festive occasions. She made me a rabbit parka and she made cotton parkas with a lining. My oldest sister told me about being a woman. She scared me by saying that I'll be getting a period and will have babies if I go with a man. She told me before I had it and she showed me how to use Kotex or Tampax. I was thirteen when I had my first period. Mostly my sister helped me. There are four girls in my family; there were five of us, but the youngest died when she 21. She was always getting sick from some hemorrhages and nose bleeds and she was always going into the hospital.

I went to school in Barrow. Then we transferred to Barter Island and I went to school there—Wainwright Institute. We learned about outside living [outside Alaska]. I ran for girls' dorm president and I won. But I missed being with my family. There was no mom or dad hugging you. It was institutionalized. The food wasn't so bad because we ate that kind of food [at home] with my mom because of my grandfather. She taught us never to be ashamed of speaking our Eskimo language. My two boys know a few common words like *Ailee* [ouch]. I was nineteen when I had my first child. I breast fed the first one for four months, but not the second one.

My mother had cervical cancer. They didn't know about it until she had a stroke and was on her death bed. They didn't do any surgical procedure. But she died of cervical cancer, too, because she was always in a lot of pain. My dad had an accident when he was getting my mom ready for the nursing home; he was hit by a car driven by a fourteen-year-old boy. So he died before she did. My mom was happy that he died ahead of her because she worried about him. He froze when there was any emergency.

My brother, older than me, had colon cancer at the same time I had breast cancer in 1990. He had radiation and surgery. He is OK. He is hunting now. I can't think of any other one in my family who had cancer.

I found my own lump. We were staying in a motel in Colorado getting ready to move into our new house. It was cold in that house and I put my hand under my night shirt and I felt this great jagged thing. It was ugly. It was hard. I didn't talk about it for a few weeks—I was terrified. I knew about breast cancer because I worked in the hospital. I called my doctor for a prescription for a mammogram. Then I went to see a breast cancer surgeon. He took a biopsy with a needle. He told me if its blood then its cancer; if its clear, it is not—and it came out blood. My husband was with me. When he [the doctor] took the needle out it was blood, and he said, "Oh no, it's cancer."

I was in shock and calm at the same time. I wasn't angry or crying or anything. It seemed that the nurse was waiting for this. The doctor spent a lot of time talking to me. I had turkey in the oven cooking, so I said to the doctor, "Are you done? My turkey is burning." The nurse just looked at me. I grew up with a strong faith in God. [She wears a cross on her hat.]

I had my surgery in Anchorage to be with my family. At first I felt as if I was missing something and a part of me was gone. I was scared to look at it, but my husband took care of that and my husband wasn't skittish about it or did not show remorse. [Because he had changed her bandages and her tubes and had seen her scar, Maxine felt that he "wasn't really bothered" when they made love for the first time after her surgery.] I had chemo for six months in Colorado and I was clean until seventeen months ago when I had a side attack, a pain, and thought it was gall bladder, but on the biopsy it came to [be cancer of] the liver. Then I went to Seattle, to University of Washington Hospital, to see if I would be a good candidate for an experimental treatment of massive doses [of chemo]. It would just make me sick. I prayed that I wouldn't go there. I went down to look at it and the patients looked deathly sick. After four months of weekly treatments, I found out that it didn't work and so I was kicked out of that research program. Then I went on Taxol. They checked once a month. I had a CAT scan after two treatments and in two months the tumor was 50 percent reduced. In July and August [1993] I was still on the treatment. I had a lot of side effects, but nothing major. By November I was having headaches. I was telling my friends and husband, "I think it's a tumor." So now I have tumors in a couple of places [in the brain] and they were treated in Providence Hospital [in Anchorage] for five weeks—radiation treatment. So each time I lucked out that they were treatable and curable.

After a month, I went back on Taxol. Each time I get checked out, and the last time he couldn't feel anything in the liver. One [tumor] came back and invaded the brain and I just got treated in June for that. After thirty-five [radiation] treatments in the winter for the other tumor, I could only have ten treatments this time. I was getting dizzy, but I continued to drive. I didn't realize that it was dangerous. Last Saturday, a woman prayed for me and the next day I didn't have any more pressure. The pressure [edema in the brain] comes when I have too much salt because it retains the fluid.

My husband helps me the most through all of this and my two boys—they are such good kids, they make me so proud of them, and are trouble free. My friends help, too. I still work for the Anchorage School district, Kindergarten to Second Grade, tracking the Head Start program. I like counseling the native students who keep dropping out. I started with five and now I have 110 who stayed in school. Work is always a good source for healing.

My biggest fear? The scariest part was how I felt after my mom and dad died, especially my dad. It was so sudden and it left such a big pain and they were such good parents, and always interested in their grand kids. That is the same fear I have for my boys and my husband. I feel so sorry for them that if anything happens to me, they will have such a big pain. That first year is so tough and the second year is tough, too. But by the beginning of the third year, they remember the good times and that is the beginning of healing. My religion has sustained me a lot. I say Holy Spirit, "Take me where you want me to be. So and so needs clothes, so and so needs food." And that blesses me and that is part of healing. I would tell other native women not to be scared. Doctors can tell you that usually when breast cancer moves to the liver that is the end of the story. Don't accept it. He [the doctor] is amazed that I am still here. If you accept it, you are going along with what the Man tells you. Jesus says, "I can do all things," and I strongly believe in that. Miracles happen. It was painful in my liver and there was times when I lived on pain killers. The pain gets so overwhelming.

I am on steroids to keep the pressure down and I take Motrin to sleep because steroids keep me charged up. I am getting my embroidery done now! We continue life! My son just graduated from law school and my in-laws came to the graduation. My father-in-law is eighty-five and we had a get together down there. The sun always shines in Colorado where he graduated. For native women, it is important to have a support group. I didn't have a strong need for that because I have a big family and lots of friends. Those people who are isolated in villages really need to get together to form a support group. It really helps. From Barrow, they send women from there to here for mammogram, but they have to feel the tumor first. Unless they know the women are at risk, like my sister. I kept pressuring her. Then they will give a screening mammogram. But otherwise, they have to feel the lump first.

During the course of my treatment, I have had mammograms. It's funny, I had felt a quarter size or dime size lump two years before I discovered the big one. I had a private doctor that I was going to in Providence Hospital for a mammogram, but when they found out I didn't have insurance, I just didn't bother. [Because Maxine is an Alaska Native, she could have had a free mammogram at Alaska Native Hospital, but didn't take advantage of this service. No reason was given.] It took 18 months for it to grow. My friend had one, too, about the same time and the doctor said that it was nothing. She yelled at them, "Take it out, take it out!" It turned out to be breast cancer. I wish I had them take mine out, too. [We discuss the fact that the government doesn't spend much money on breast cancer research, especially for native people, "They only spend 5 percent on breast cancer research, but they have money to spend on bombs and defense." We talk about my own family's breast cancer and how I deal with that threat.] Women must not resign their fate, they must fight back. I am looking forward to school to start, so that I can forget a lot of this. I think your attitude has a lot to do with getting well. I've seen women who have had cancer; you can see it in their face, that they have accepted it.

Interview Analysis

Maxine discussed health care in native villages in the North. She knows more preventive screening needs to happen there, especially for women over fifty. The same mammography recommendations for women in the lower forty-eight should also apply to women currently living in native villages in Alaska. Maxine also recognizes the need for more breast cancer research. She speaks of the rising incidence of breast cancer especially since 1969. Although Maxine suffered after her surgery, feeling like half a woman, not wanting to look at her scar, she did respond well to her husband who was with her every step of the way, even to the changing of her bandages. Clearly, she and her husband held a real partnership in her healing. When she was diagnosed in 1990 in the lower forty-eight and then told the news, her husband was with her. Maxine has great faith in her religion, which has also helped her. Spirituality and the love of her family have sustained her. Although in stage four with metastasis to her brain and liver, Maxine thinks of others, like her sons and her husband, before thinking of herself. Her positive attitude helps her to question everything that the doctor tells her, and she continues to fight for her life. Maxine has good insight into the supportive nature of groups with other breast cancer women. Our meeting was a happy one with much laughing. For someone who has had such suffering, Maxine demonstrates power, strength, love, and trust. She is an inspiration to me. [Maxine died two months after our interview.]

Fiona

Of all the women I interviewed, Fiona is unique. She is the only woman who voluntarily presented her mastectomy scars. "See? Like a boy," she said. Fiona has blended her traditional Inupiat culture with that of the lower forty-eight. She is married for the second time to a seventy-four-year-old Caucasian man. Recently, they remodeled their modest home ("with my Eskimo money") situated on a suburban street in Anchorage. When I called to set up the interview, Fiona told me how to identify her house. "It's the one with all the trees!" Their big, mixed-breed floppy dog and chain-link kennel dominates one portion of the yard. Tomatoes, vegetables, and flowers are everywhere else. Both Fiona and her husband smoke pot, cigarettes, and consume alcohol. On the day we met, she told me that she just smoked pot to relieve her nervousness about the interview. Fiona is fifty-seven-years-old and was born in Point Hope, Alaska, "up on the tundra." Since coming to Anchorage, she has developed many allergies to the trees. We sit telling stories in her dimly lighted kitchen at the brown, wooden table. There are two chairs.

Fiona's Story

> I come from the tundra. When I got here, I started to sneeze and my eyes watered. I am one of thirteen children and was born at Point Hope in 1937, but I left home in 1957 to go to high school at Mt. Edgecombe. There were seven hundred kids there. We spoke our language in the dorms [she was philosophical about this, English being the only language allowed in class]. They was gettin' us ready for the world.
>
> I always stay home now since my surgery. The sun really bothers me and I don't go out durin' the day. I got my first period when I was thirteen. I stayed in bed. I didn't know what it was. After my first period, my mother told me, "You are a woman." She also told me about having babies and all of that. But my grandmother taught me the traditional ways. I never learned the traditional crafts. I am the oldest and the only one who had cancer.
>
> I got married at nineteen. My husband was always abusing me [physical beatings/spousal abuse]. We had two boys. I call them my little Indians. Their father was a Tsimshian Indian. Because I had TB, I didn't breast feed them. My father and an infant sister also died of TB.

I had six kids all together. They all eat Eskimo foods, fish head chowder, especially the eyeballs and cheeks, seals, duck soup. But I was an abused wife. I had a hysterectomy. My husband drank a lot. So I left him. I have a very supportive second husband, a "White man." I just gave him a seventy-fourth birthday party. That is the cake I made [a huge chocolate sheet cake, that made my mouth water!]. I found my own lump, but I kept it a secret for six months. I was leanin' over the couch to get a kid's toy and I had this pain. Then I told my friend who is a health aide. She told me to go get it checked out, that it was probably a cyst, but my friend knew it was cancer, too. I think my mother died of cancer too [she wasn't sure of the site]. It wasn't breast cancer.

My husband was OK after my surgery. I asked him to suck my falsie, my false tittie, but he wouldn't. But he sucked the other one. [Fiona was very open with this and she was laughing and joking around. She lifted up her shirt to show me her scars from the TB and from her surgery. It was a clean scar, without extra tissue growth. Her breast looked empty, and concave, like a boy's.] When I went through chemo, I thought that I'd die. I would go to the chemo, come out, get in the car and open the door and throw up in the street. Sometimes I'd just go have beer to make me feel better. I smoked pot a lot before I went in. All my hair fell out; my skin peeled; my nails got dark. It took a long time to feel better. While I was in the hospital having surgery, my sutures got infected and I was so sick. I had my surgery on December 23rd and I went home for Christmas. My sutures got infected and I had a hard time. My grand kids helped me, getting me things and staying with me. I prayed a lot every night, to a greater being. When I felt better, I cleaned the house to get the sickness out.

Since I had chemo, my hair has grown in black. Look at this hair [as she ran her fingers through it; she is very proud of her hair and skin; she is beautiful] and my skin is smooth. See, there are no wrinkles. I look good. I just have this rash on my hands. I put seal oil on it and it is getting better. I have my mamm-y-o-gram ever year at the Alaska Native Hospital women's clinic. My greatest fear is gettin' it again.

[Fiona is mindful of current events in cancer research. We discuss the nuclear contamination of the caribou in Cape Thompson.] The caribou go through there [on migration] and they get sick. They have dark spots on their meat. You can't eat it. The whales go through there, too [and become sick]. I am so angry with the White people for doing this. Why don't they clean it up? [Fiona is aware that there is a link between smoking and alcohol and cancer, and she suspects that there is a link

between what is happening to the whales and caribou and cancer.] My
mother was the oldest and she got it, and I am the oldest.

I have a good life. I read the scandal sheets and about O. J. Simp-
son. I work in my garden. Claudette [the nurse in the chemo department at Alaska Native Hospital] was so good to me. I would tell other
women to let others teach you about what is going on. Have the will to
live. Be strong to take care of your kids. I was in denial for six months.
Get checked out right away.

Interview Analysis

I am utterly amazed by the hardships that consume the lives of so many
northern women, even before their breast cancer diagnosis. They are
strong. Fiona demonstrates that strength in surviving spousal abuse and
breast cancer with the will to endure. As in the tradition of Inupiat survival skills, where Inupiats adopted certain artifacts and behaviors from
other cultures, Fiona has accepted Western adaptations of pot and alcohol
to assist in her coping strategies for cancer. She feels a sense of well-being
in her life and satisfaction with her marriage. During our interview, she received a call from Claudette reminding her to "be nice and cooperative."
After the call, she told me that she has a reputation for being nasty, but
wants to help other Native Women, so she will be "nice to me." She knows
that our work together will help others. She is a powerful woman, aware of
environmental contamination, and the possible cancer link. She is angry
about the White people polluting Alaska.

Glenda: 1994

Proud of her degree in Business from San Francisco State [now San
Francisco State University], Glenda is a modern Inupiat woman living in her
own condominium and managing the rest of the buildings. She is slim,
works out at the gym, and has left her breast cancer experience behind her.

Glenda's Story

I grew up in Unalakeleet, Alaska, basically a small village located right
on the Bering Straits. There was about 600 people there. When I was
growing up and up until I was fourteen or fifteen we didn't have running

water or any of the luxuries. Everyone in the village was basically poor. It was a tough life, but OK, I guess. My junior and senior year I went to Mt. Edgecombe [high school]. Then I moved to California after that and spent most of my adult life in California. I was educated in California and, of course, I went back and forth [to Alaska]. California is like a big melting pot. No one there asks "What are you?"

My mother and father worked for years. My father was the Magistrate. My mother was a teacher's aide. My Dad retired at age sixty-nine. My mother just retired. They pushed education. I have two sisters that graduated from Stanford. I come from that kind of a family. My dad used to hunt, but as I was growing up, we ate store food and dried fish. It helps a lot to eat traditional food.

They [her parents] didn't let us eat the real native food. They thought that we'd get sick. My dad is half German and my mom has some British.

I could have married a very wealthy man from New York, but I couldn't see myself in New York. I never got married. And I never had any children. I was thirteen when I had my first period, but chemo's knocked that out [now]. If I took some steroids, I could have it [a period] but I don't miss it. My grandmother died a couple of years ago [of breast cancer]. She was an interesting person. She grew up in the olden days. A couple of aunts who teaches up there [in Northern Alaska] had breast cancer and had breast implants put in and so did her daughter. Then I had another aunt, who is traveling now, had one [breast] off, then another. My mother lost the right side and went for reconstruction. She is fine. I am the only one of my six sisters who developed breast cancer. I am the oldest.

My surgery was two or three years ago. Because I didn't have insurance, I couldn't go to Stanford. At first he was going to do an excision and radiation, but I had two nodes that were positive. I went in [to the surgery] happy. I had been a vegetarian and worked out. Like an idiot, I listened to the two doctors at Stanford who recommended mastectomy. I flew back here to Alaska Native Hospital to have it done here [in Anchorage]. The plastic surgeon said right after chemo, when I was in a haze, that I should have the other side done, too. I had the other side done and I never should have. A lumpectomy would have done the job. I don't think that it would have recurred. I made a mistake and I wish I could go back, but I can't. I had reconstruction. They look like grapefruits. I was in great shape before. I am going to have the saline implants when they become available. I am concerned about the silicone.

I was by myself when they told me about the tumor. I was devastated. The doctor came in and they were laughing outside the door. Then he opened the door and told me. I felt like they were laughing at me [before they came in the door]. The oncologist was nasty. I told him that I was going to be fine. He said angrily to me, "How do you know?"

I do now. I have relationships with men but I don't have to explain the fact that I have had a mastectomy. The fear that people have worries me. I am a healthy person.

I used to go to support group, but a lady who also went had a recurrence and it felt that she was expecting to have it. She sat next to me and I could smell her chemo. I stopped going. I pushed myself to be well when I was on chemo. I didn't lose my hair. I am physically healthy and I stopped going to the support group. It put the fear back in me. You can talk yourself into things and talk yourself out of them. I am my own best therapy. Between God and the medicine, I am healed. My sisters helped, but we never talked about it. It was like, "Get on with your life. It happened and now it is over."

To other women I would say, "Breast cancer is a terrible thing; it is scary. There is research going on and don't let anyone talk you into anything. Do the research. Check out your options. You will be strengthened by it." I have heard of Tamoxifen, but there is no reason for me to take it. I take Nature's Way Vitamins.

Interview Analysis

Glenda's modern condominium is far from the small village in the Arctic where she was raised. Because of her contacts while she was in college in California, her Inupiat culture has blended with that of the southern part of North America. Sitting on her black leather sofa, she offers me coffee from her Mr. Coffee or a heated roll from her microwave. Still, her connection to her culture is evident from the many paintings of Inupiat life created by a friend of her grandfather's: large paintings of Inupiat village life full of friends that her grandfather knew as a young man. Glenda's home is furnished with stylish, overstuffed, black leather sofas. Glenda is extremely proud of her education and her home. She has accomplished much. Surviving breast cancer is only one of the many special things that she has mastered. Putting her breast cancer behind her, she is cheerful now and open with me. To the men she dates, she doesn't "broadcast the fact" that she has had breast cancer, but her lifestyle has changed. Her diet is more nutritious and she is aware of the importance of vitamins and the damage that eating red meat can cause. She dates, continues to work out at the gym, and is looking forward to returning to school for a master's degree. I ask her about getting married. "I haven't found the right one yet, but I don't want to spend my whole life taking care of a man," she responds quickly.

Rubra: 1994

Rubra is a Haida and Italian woman who calls herself "The Mouth." She was diagnosed with her cancer at age thirty-five. Her husband was murdered soon after her surgery. She is approaching forty and is angry at how she has come to this situation in her life. Because she is going home to her people on the southwest islands of Alaska, she is anxious for me to meet with her before her trip. No one else in her family has had breast cancer. She feels that she "got it" because she is the only one in her family who could deal with it. She is strong.

In her modern apartment, evidence of her Haida heritage are everywhere, from the *Chilkat* robe* made of wool to paintings of Raven and wall hangings and carvings. She greets me warmly and is anxious to tell me her story. We sit together on her couch; it is as if I am visiting with a classmate from high school. But when Rubra speaks, she is articulate; her speech is clipped and filled with anger.

Rubra's Story

I was born in Hydaburg, but when I was six or seven we moved to Ketchican. It was in the summer or early spring we went for a visit and I was walking up from the dock [in Hydaburg] and I thought it was the most beautiful place I had ever seen in my life because there were

---

*Chilkat blanket/robe: Ceremonial robe made of mountain goat wool created by Haida and Tsimshian women for high-ranking people. In the old days it took a master weaver one year to create the robe on an upright loom. The warp is made of spun cedar and pure white mountain goat wool. The weft is made of pure white and dyed yellow, black blue-green mountain goat wool (Taylor, 1995, p. 97).

salmonberry blossoms and everything was green. I thought I was in heaven; it was a kid's paradise; it was wild and free and green, there were no boundaries. In Ketchican we had to walk to school—it was entirely different. That [Ketchican] was my first encounter with older kids. At Halloween the kids stole our candy. In Hydaburg, it was my whole family, about 300 people.

Now there are quite a few tourists who come to Hydaburg because it is so beautiful with lots of wildlife everywhere. My mother teaches Haida arts and crafts and song and dance. I think it should be taught before any other culture is taught to us because it is our culture; it is who we are; if we don't know about Haida, we are wandering around empty and have no meaning and no direction in our lives. When I was going to school, I went to Ketchican up to eighth grade and then to a boarding school, a high school in Salem, Oregon, at Chemawa. My mother could never teach us Haida because they [the government] tried to erase everything [language and culture] from her generation. They tried with my mother to erase all of that. But it was still there hidden somewhere—remembered. It was never taught to our generation.

The girls at the reservation [Chemawa high school in Oregon] thought we were rich and too good for the reservation. We [in Alaska] never knew what reservations were. The food was gross; fried and lots of fat. In Hydaburg we had lots of boiled fish. I hated the taste of the grease. It left a bad taste in my mouth, like a coating.

My grandmother taught us how to care for the fish. We had to do everything seasonally. Our family was always like that. Me and my sister Toni had to clean fish while other kids were playing and swimming in the creek; we hurried to lug the fish or seal meat up to the smoke house. My grandmother was influential in my life and that is why I am sitting here today because of the values she taught us. My mom was gone a lot. In my village we were always getting in fights and getting challenged. I never let people beat me up. We lived on one end of the town and my brothers who were getting in trouble had to go to Haines [to a youth detention center]. There was a lot of alcohol. I went from my aunts to my grandmother and I never knew where I was going to be. I had to grow from those changes.

I was the one who taught me about being a woman. I learned the hard way. I was fourteen when I had my first period. I learned about sex the hard way. I was nineteen when I had my first experience and that is my daughter, Haida. I was in College in Seattle, a business college, and met this man who was extremely handsome and also a Haida, but raised in California [the White way], so he didn't even know what it meant [to be a Haida]. I don't know how we ended up together. People encouraged me to have an abortion; you're too young, but I couldn't do that. I would be like taking part of me and killing it. I have three children, two girls and a boy. I named my first girl Haida Raven. I was so proud of myself and the values that my grandmother gave me. I remember all the old ladies used to sit on the steps and talk in a mixture of English and Haida. My traditional values have brought me back to who I am.

I have seven brothers and sisters. Some live in Hydaburg, some are teachers in eastern Washington. One brother died of drowning fifteen years ago. I named my son after him, Billy. No one else in my family has had cancer of the breast. My aunt has cancer, stomach cancer. She died of it because of too much drinking. My uncle died of throat cancer. I would like to know more of my father's [Italian] side of the family; it is a great mystery, like I'm not whole. I'll probably spend the next forty years finding out about that side of the family. My *Non* [Italian word for grandmother, but also a Haida word. Rubra is talking about her Haida grandmother] is still alive, my grandfather, just passed away, was a chief. My grandmother wasn't married when she had my mom; she was real young. Then she got married and my mother got her name. My mother's father was a chief! My father died years ago, but I don't know of what.

The pollution is all over, not just in the Arctic. There have been forty to fifty people from my area that have died of breast cancer. Fortunately, I am still here—maybe because I am so young and I fight and have the will to live. I wasn't going to let anybody take me out like that. All of our water is polluted and the food chain is contaminated. It contaminates the people who eat it. We have had to change our food, too, because of state regulations for tourism. They [the government] would rather have someone die so that a tourist can take a fish. They have to spray our vegetables and fruit to keep the bugs off. And then we have to eat it. If you eat, it causes cancer.

I found the lump in my breast. I was in Petersburg. I was married for six months and my husband was working there with the Fish and Wildlife, building generators for the hatchery so they could have more fish. We were laying on the floor because we didn't have a couch and I was touching my breast. I kept feeling kind of weird because I would bleed and the doctors were giving me birth control pills to regulate the bleeding. I went to the doctor in Petersburg and he sent me to Ketchican where I got my mammogram results. All I could think of was how am I going to say this to my husband [that I had breast cancer]? The doctor told me that he made a phone call to be on the jet tonight and have surgery tomorrow. I was alone when the doctor told me that I had breast cancer. I refused to believe him. I left his office with the mammogram X-ray and went to the bar and got totally smashed because I didn't want to believe what he just said. That was in November before my thirty-fourth birthday. I had been getting pains in my breast for a while and I went to the doctor [another doctor] and she told me that one of my breasts was different from the other. She told me that it was like an orange peeling, but didn't refer me to get the mammogram because she said I was too young. She kept giving me birth control pills. I imagine that the birth control pill was making it [the cancer] grow fast. I could tell by my nails two years before that something was wrong. I went to cosmetology school where I learned that if anything was wrong internally, it would show on the nails first. My nails started to go from flat and smooth to ridged. I was dealing with Alaska Native Health and the federal government. As far as I'm concerned, if you look at the country and see how that is run, the health service can't be run any better. It isn't that they just don't catch it; they don't know what they are looking for. How can you have an adequate health service and have so many sick people? We all know that it isn't well run.

When I left Petersburg to go for surgery [in Ketchican], I convinced my husband to stay in Petersburg to keep his job and I went to Ketchican. I still didn't believe I had it [breast cancer]. Why me of all the people that I know? There isn't anyone as young as me that had breast cancer. I saw the mammogram. It was white all over and I had this big mass. I freaked. I went through this period full of anger and bitterness, then I said to myself, "You have it because you're the only one that can pull it off. That way, since it's me, anyone can survive." It was a week before I got my act together and my kids situated. I was still in shock. I couldn't believe it. It was too devastating. I didn't want to hear the word. It was my breast, not only cancer, but breast cancer, and I was thirty-four-years old and just married and they were going to remove my breast. I was totally freaked out. Then, as I thought about it, things worked out. I had love and felt what that was like, and I was married and felt what that was like. Then I had breast cancer and tried to recover from it. The worst part was trying to get myself up from this fall.

I secluded myself for a whole year and found out who my friends were. They thought that I was so vain and that I would die. My husband was wonderful. We were really in love. We got married a week after we met. He said that it didn't matter, but what I didn't know was that he had already gone through this with another woman who had his son and died of it. How can God punish him twice by putting him through this again? That's what hurt me the most—he was so hurt because I was so hurt. I could see it and it really bothered me. I told him to go find another woman, one that he could have children with, but that's not what he was about. That's when I learned who he really was. He said that it didn't matter, but to me it did. I felt like I was denying him [a breast] and that was really selfish.

[Rubra's husband was shot and murdered soon after she went through chemo. It is painful for Rubra to talk about this part of her life and she denied me any information. She did tell me, however that several of her friends think that she had her husband killed and that is what hurts her so much. When she composed herself, we continued.] It is a part of me that will never go away [his murder].

I had six months of chemo. I took pot to alleviate the nausea. I had it in Ketchican. I was so sick the first time I threw up for eight hours. My veins all collapsed. My husband got angry because they told him to get me a wig. The woman [who was in charge of the chemo department] had been doing it [giving chemo] for so long and she didn't even think about my feelings. The first thing—to get a wig before I even start! My husband was so angry at her. He told her, "She isn't going to lose her hair."

I used pot to save me. "Go," I told W_____, "look on the streets and get me enough for six months." He would be in the room [where the chemo was given] and it made him sick, too, so I told him to leave the room. It was hard for him to leave me in there because I was alone, but the nurse who was in there was wonderful and it made all the difference. After the treatment, I would run to the car for some pot. I didn't lose my hair. It was the only thing that saved me for six months. I told my friend whose mother had cancer to give her mother pot, but she wouldn't. The doctor asked me what I was doing because something was different about my treatment. I told him that I was taking pot. Someone told my mom to send me to Greece to Dr. Alvizar for cancer treatments. It was over $8,000 to send me. My family and friends had dinners and raffles to raise the money. They raised the money in a month and a half.

Interview Analysis

Rubra's mother had reservations about Rubra going to Greece, because of the war and political unrest in the Middle East, but Rubra was insistent and told her mother that she was going to Greece to save herself. Rubra put her trust in God and went to Greece to seek an unusual immune system treatment for her cancer. As Rubra described her treatment, she *thinks* it involved intravenous application of "Vitamin C and other vitamins and herbs." It is a procedure which is not currently recognized in the United States by the Federal Drug Administration.

Although Rubra was unable to describe specifically what was in her treatment in Greece, she did describe in detail her quest to help herself. When Rubra arrived in Seattle on her way to Athens, she went to her Aunt Louise. Aunt Louise was always accepting and forgiving of Rubra. When Louise opened the door, she said to Rubra, "I knew you were coming." She wanted the priest to bless her, which Rubra allowed. After the blessing, Rubra put all of her faith in God. It hurt her Aunt Louise to let her go to Athens, but Rubra put her trust in the Lord. Because of her trust, Rubra was able to withstand the terrible turbulence over Greenland and let her faith pull her through the month-long treatments in Athens. This was the first time Rubra had ever been out of Alaska, and she was awed by the whiteness, heat, and panorama of Athens itself.

While in Athens, Rubra underwent treatment for her immune system. She believes that cancer is a deficiency in the immune system. Among medical researchers the idea that cancer is caused by immune deficiency is controversial. However, Boik (1995, p. 58) believes that there is a link and that natural agents such as herbs, melatonin,* and thymostimulin[†] can stimulate the immune system.

---

*Melatonin: a hormone produced by the pituitary gland in mammals.
[†]Thymostimulin: an agent that stimulates the thymus to produce T cells, important in the body's cellular immune response.

The importance of immune defenses against cancer remains a matter of great controversy. One school of thought argues that specialized cells in the immune system continuously survey cells for nests of tumor cells that, once recognized, are attacked and wiped out. This view is supported by the discovery of natural killer (NK) lymphocytes that seem to identify and destroy many types of tumor cells. If immune surveillance by these and other cell types is indeed important in antitumordefenses, then cancer cells must acquire an ability to elude the immune system. (Varmus & Weinberg, 1993, p. 178)

Apparently many other lay people believe in the efficacy of this controversial treatment, and Rubra describes the facility in Greece as crowded with patients from all over the world. As the discussion proceeds, she talks of all the other patients—young, old, even children—who went to Athens to seek immune system treatment. The treatment lasts for a month and burned her body all over in the places where the cancer was. Rubra describes how her whole body turned red after each treatment and that none of her flesh could come in contact with her other flesh, otherwise it would be too painful.

Because of the number of patients seen in the clinic each day, the doctor never made eye contact or spoke with the patients. In Rubra's words, he just "had them stick out their arm and he injected the serum into them." During all of the treatments, as well, the clinic kept track of her blood counts in order to determine how many more treatments were needed.

As a child, Rubra used to spit at everything, so she put her cancer in her mind and decided that she would spit the cancer out. She drank seven liters of water a day in order to flush out the cancer from her body. Today, Rubra drinks special all natural herbal medicines called Sunrider. But her culture and her faith have made her strong.

Rubra's Story: Further

To other women who have breast cancer, I would tell them don't worry about things that you cannot change, only the things that you can control. Every night I pray for everyone, children of the world who have no food or clothes to wear; nothing in life is worth your health. You are responsible for yourself, things that you can change, you can change; and the things that you can't change, don't worry about them. I used to carry around lots of stuff in my mind, things like incest, child abuse, that sort of thing. Now those things don't bother me.

Cancer has made me stronger. No one is going to hurt me anymore. I enjoy my life even though it is rough: I am OK. Breast cancer has made me strong like I am at the top of a mountain where no one can get me. Sometimes I don't feel whole, but I know that there isn't anyone else in the world like me. I got it because I can deal with it!

Rubra's Story: Interview Analysis Continued

Rubra is independent and appears very strong. All of her life she has had to fight for the things that have made her whole, her culture, her love of the land and of people. She has turned to her own Haida values and matrilineal culture to help her get through her breast cancer. Her apartment is filled with artifacts that bespeak her culture: a Chilkat robe made of wool in the traditional yellow and black colors covers her sofa; other paintings of eagles and ravens done in the Haida style fill the walls. She is a survivor, a risk taker, and a pioneer willing to accept alternative treatments such as immune therapy. Nonetheless, and as I have noted, there is controversy regarding the immune system's role in the treatment of cancer. The concept of immune surveillance* was first proposed by Erlich (1909) and is supported by Penn (1991). However, while "the immune system may limit carcinogenesis by destroying newly transformed cells, and may limit the growth of established tumors. . . . even with immunotherapy, remission and cure rates have been low" (Boik, 1995, p. 79).

Work in the 1970s and more recently has also demonstrated some evidence linking Vitamin A, C, and E by infusion to the treatment and prevention of cancer. As Cameron and Pauling (1979) point out, two studies done in 1976 and 1979 by Yonemoto, Chretien, and Fehniger did demonstrate that high intake of Vitamin C by cancer patients increases the body's protective mechanism involving lymphocytes (white blood cells), leading thereby to a more favorable prognosis for the patient. Currently, as well, the National Cancer Institute (NCI) (1996) is sponsoring

---

*Immune surveillance: the ability of the immune system to recognize and seek out tumor cells. Many of the tumor cells evade the immune system, but it does not mean that immune therapy is ineffective against them. Interferons affect a wide variety of immunological functions including the suppression of the oncogenes.

studies which experiment with vitamin C in preventing initial development of some types of cancer, but the protective mechanism is unclear and more work is needed.

One has to love Rubra for the love she feels for everything in the world. Her problems are her own, but she still has time to help her friends, to have a boyfriend, and to share her place with other women. Rubra has been honest in the interview, revealing much about her marijuana experiences and hinting at childhood traumas of incest and abuse for those who would continue to unravel the secrets that are Rubra's.

I was honored to have interviewed Rubra. We are in a similar age range. It is frightening to meet one so young who has been challenged in so many ways. I am taken in by the strength of her bravery. After the interview, Rubra received a phone call from a friend, and I detected pride and empowerment in her voice when she told the person on the other end of the phone, "I'm being interviewed right now. You know, because I survived breast cancer. We are making a documentary video!"

Linda: 1994

A graduate of Gonzaga University in Spokane with a BS in Biology, Linda is the personification of the Haida matrilineal influence. Both Linda's daughters have achieved academically, one as an attorney now living in Arizona, the other as a computer analyst. As a mother, Linda is extremely proud of their educational status. Linda's grandmother, mother, and several other family members have had breast cancer. Currently, Linda works as a laboratory technician in one of Anchorage's hospitals, and prior to that as a college teacher in chemistry. Linda owns her own home and lives with her only grandson. She is the epitome of the modern Haida woman and, at fifty-nine, a role model for her people. We meet in her living room. She is wearing a black top and pants. It is dark in the room except for a small reading lamp. Linda is quite obese despite the impression created by the presence of exercise equipment.

Linda's Story

We were in several villages while I was growing up. My mother worked as a cannery worker and my father was a commercial fisherman. I was born in Craig [Alaska]. Most of my childhood I was brought up in Ketchican. Craig is quite vague to me. I remember my grandmother in Craig. She was a woman! Her name was Matilda and I remember staying with her and helping her with her beads; she was always humming or whistling and my mother was the same, always whistling. My mother might have been thirty when we were in Craig. Going to school in Ketchican was hard on me because I was so very native. I was the first generation [in my family] who was allowed to go to public school. I could run pretty fast. I had to—the white kids would wait for us and they wanted to hit us. There were ten thousand people there. I went to Mount Edgecombe High School. I spent one year in high school in Ketchican. Mount Edgecombe was very poor education. I had to struggle [there] to get the background for college.

I don't speak my language. My mother was not allowed to teach us Haida. My children were raised in Wisconsin and they don't speak it either.

Going to college was very difficult for me. I went to Gonzaga University in Spokane. It was a pretty tough university. I was never treated differently [racially] any time that I was out of Alaska. Today, though, especially today, it's a subtle thing, but it's always there. I went to rent an apartment [in Anchorage]. I called on the telephone and I don't have an accent, but the apartment was not available when I arrived. Now I live it all the time [prejudice]. I have two daughters. She doesn't look native; she is a computer analyst with Marathon Oil. Her friends who don't know she is native put down natives to her. Sometimes she tells them off and sometimes she doesn't. It exists on my job, too, and it is painful.

When I worked in Wisconsin, I taught college graduates and they knew what a good teacher I was. They don't utilize me here. I don't pursue it. Being an instructor is important to me more than being a supervisor. I rotate in the blood bank as a tech. I majored in biology and minored in chemistry. I don't let those things concern me any more.

My mother taught me all about being a woman. I don't remember how old I was when I had my period, but I got it at Girl Scout camp. My mother told me before I had my period in words that were meaningful for me at the time. She is a remarkable woman. I was married at twenty-one and I had a child when I was twenty-two almost twenty-three. I couldn't breast feed—because of a strange phenomenon that was happening to me. The doctors advised against it. I have five brothers and three sisters. My sister had bilateral breast cancer. She was very young. But she died from cancer of the pancreas and liver. She was pregnant when she had the second breast removed. They wanted her to abort her baby. She was in her thirties. We had quite a bit of cancer. My mother and her mother had breast cancer and my mother's sister had it. They all died. My father died of rectal cancer. His brother died of leukemia. One sister died of breast cancer. One had liver cancer. His two sisters died of breast cancer.

My daughters are so conscientious about their health. I don't worry about them. I am in my fifth year [of survival]. It will be five years this November. I was in the shower getting ready for work. It [my breast] felt like I was going to have my period and it was painful. I felt the lump and I was very alarmed. I went in as "walk in" to ANS [Alaska Native Hospital] and they set up appointments for me to see a surgeon. I was pretty terrified from the family history—no one has survived. My very good friend was with me when they told me. She was pretty sure that I was positive [and went with her]. My cancer was stage one and my lymph nodes were negative. They came to me and told me that they were negative and that I didn't have to have chemo. That was wonderful! I was very happy, of course. But when I went home and thought about it, it concerned me. There are brand new publications out about node-negative women having chemo. I talked with some pathologists in Wisconsin that I knew and I went to see another doctor here for advice. We talked about it for an hour and she said if it were her, she would have chemo. I went to talk to them at ANS and they were upset, but I felt that I should take every step that I could.

I was in chemo for six months. It was pretty horrible. Claudette [the nurse] gave me the chemo once a week. She is a very kind woman. I had nausea, diarrhea, burning stomach. I had Candida in my mouth. It is pretty uncomfortable. I took real high doses of prednisone. They shut down the immune system. That is the worst way to treat cancer—to shut down the immune system. I think that you should treat it nutritionally for one thing, so it will help the immune system.

Multiple studies (Peto et al., 1981; Sporn, 1983; Hennekens, 1986; Menkes, 1986) have been done on the effects of antioxidents and B vitamins on immunity. Their studies demonstrate that certain nutrients can enhance the immune system, protect against free radicals,* protect against carcinogens, and hence protect normal cells from transforming into malignant cells. (Simone, 1992)

In chemo you are treating the system. The disease is the fault of the immune system. We all make cancer cells every day. [This is Linda's view as a biologist. I interpret this to mean: humans have cells which have the potential to become cancerous if it weren't for the newly discovered oncogene that regulates cell growth. If the oncogene is defective, cells may grow out of control as tumors.] We need our immune system, too. I also went to Greece to Dr. Alvizar. All I eat now are grains and bananas and drink tons of water. The restrictions make sense to me. I had to stick with that for six months. I use herbs and the *Sunrider*—it's done a lot for me. I used to have sinus headaches. I used to take sinus medication every day and [now] I don't. I used to have high blood pressure. It also helped my eczema. Diet plays a big role in cancer. There is so much pollution with pesticides. It is really a serious matter. I go to Enzyme Express in town and try to have one or two of those a week and stay away from prepared foods. I eat lots of fish. I had a simple mastectomy. I did go to Greece. What they did with the chemo is to shut the immune system down and I had this high cancer cell count in the lymph system, so I went to Greece.

The food at the hospital is terrible—the grease and the salt. Emotionally, my family had a lot to do with it [my recovery]. The people that I work with give me a lot of support. When I went to Greece, they raised $1,500 for me in four days.

In Hydaburg, the children drink a lot of pop and eat chips and smoke cigarettes. Maybe that's why the cancer incidence is so high there.

I would tell other women not to have a mastectomy. I would use the doctors here, and follow their advice intelligently. But I would contact someone else in Mexico who is doing the same treatment as Doctor Alvizar [in Greece]. They treat the immune system, and teach you to treat the faulty immune system. I would not have radiation or have my

---

*Free radical: chemical substances being made by the human body as a result of oxidation. The free radical atom has an odd number of electrons. Because of the odd number of electrons, the atom has high energy, is unstable, and is seeking to transfer its energy. When free radicals are made in the body, the high energy is transferred to body tissues. Free radicals can destroy the fat/lipid layer in the cell membrane (Simone, 1992).

lymph nodes removed. I would have them treat me as if they [lymph nodes] were all positive. You get lymphedema. The swelling begins [in the arm] and it is heavy.

I think that native women are neglected. There is poor communication [between them and the doctors]. I don't have a problem, because I can speak up, but what do these poor village people do? The way they treat them. . . .

I have a dysfunctional parotid gland. The doctors don't want to know anything about anything unless they feel it has something to do with my metastatic cancer. They are in a big hurry. I have had stomach problems for a month. The doctors are always in a big hurry. I can speak up. There aren't enough people like Claudette there.

I wasn't having mammogram when I was diagnosed, just [clinical] breast exams. I don't know if they are qualified to see the things in a mammogram. I have one every year now, but I didn't before. I think that a breast exam is really important, too. My friend had a mammogram and, the next year, she had a mastectomy because they didn't see the tumor on the mammogram.

The food in the hospital is non-nutritious: too much fat and too much thick gravy. We ate a lot of fish when I was growing up. When I moved to Ketchican, we moved away from our sources. My mother used to buy as much fruit as possible. We would sit around and eat all the fruit. My mother went to Chemawa in Oregon [to school]. She lied about her age to go. She wanted to go to school so badly.

My greatest fear is these stomach pains that I have, but the doctor thinks it is from stress. I have been under a lot of stress at work. Hopefully it will be resolved soon.

A positive attitude and education are really important. There is a breast cancer group that I go to. It is important to educate yourself—from those moments of terror, and that is the feeling that you have. It is something you can fight. There is a big difference in those feelings [now when I am educated]. I was stunned when I found out that it [the cancer] had spread after the chemo and everything. I am stronger, but my divorce made me stronger, too. My younger daughter J_____ has had two biopsies done; the first one was more terrifying than the last, because we all thought it was cancer. It turned out to be a cyst. She has fibrocystic disease. It isn't fair because of her family history [of breast cancer]. She is athletic and careful about what she eats. We are really close. She lives in Anchorage.

Interview Analysis

Initially in the interview, Linda's guarded, bitter and angry attitude was reflected in her conversation with me. Her anger stems from racial prejudice and the horror that it has brought to her since she has returned to Anchorage. She states that Native People are not well treated in Alaska. She had no problem racially in the lower forty-eight, only in Alaska.

As the interview proceeded, I gained her confidence. She smiled more and became more open with her answers. She relaxed and began to trust me and the process and outcome of the interview—to help educate other women. Her mother and grandmother were very influential in forming her ideas concerning education as well. In the Haida culture, women are the role models for the younger children. Linda continually mentions her daughters who are well educated in the lower forty-eight. She is obviously bright and questions authority. Her degree in biology and her assertiveness are assets in deciding her treatment options. Like Rubra, she is a risk taker and has undergone treatment in Greece as well as chemo in order to cover all of her options. Linda is a new breed of native woman, one who has been empowered by education and the independence of divorce.

Ingred: 1994

The two Athabascan women in this study lived alone and were the sole support of their children and grandchildren. They were victims of spousal abuse, divorced, and ultimately overcame their breast cancers by way of their toughness. They carry the burden of many native women—abused wife, single parent, head of the household, and breast cancer survivor.

Tucked into a pocket of poverty near Anchorage's busiest roadways, Ingred lives in a rickety old trailer. Her work as a hospital housekeeper provides the things that her family needs. During the time of the visit, her family consisted of her youngest son and several visiting grandchildren. Ingred is quiet but also tense and nervous. I can see by her behavior and body language that she wants the interview to pass quickly. Relations between us are strained in spite of my attempts to improve the situation. I ask her about her work and any cultural activities she enjoys. Disclosing my family's history of breast cancer, I search for a common bond.

We sit at her kitchen table, where on an oilcloth Ingred studies homework for her job out of a black, loose-leaf binder. She sleeps early and rises at 5:00 A.M. to begin her day. She is proud that she can bead in the tradition of her people; she also speaks her own language. Ingred, who is the only informant who refused to sign the consent form for the interview, did give me a verbal consent to ask her questions. She is just fifty years old.

Ingred's Story

I remember the building of the ALCAN highway that came through my village of Circle. My father worked on the highway. That road is winding and they straightened it out. There were only about a hundred people who lived in the village at that time. My mother taught me to tan moose hides, sew moccasins and to sew the beads, but I never made the moccasins. [She smiles and states proudly] I still can speak my own Athabascan language. I went to a one room school in Circle. There were about 20 kids in grade one to eight. When we were kids we used to eat fish, ducks, moose, rabbit, and geese. My brother used to hunt. We also went to pick berries. I was twelve when I had my first period. I had it for two weeks. Then it was regular. I think that my menopause is starting. My older sister told me about being a woman.

There are twelve in my family. I am the second youngest. One of my sisters had uterine cancer and her son had stomach cancer and died around age forty. My mother died of a stroke. She had high blood pressure. My Dad is eighty-eight and is still living. He is in good shape. I have three kids, two boys and a girl. I have three grandchildren. I was twenty-one when I had my first child.

The doctor found the lump when I went for a housekeeping job [at Alaska Native Hospital] and they gave me a physical for the job in 1988. The doctor told me [I had breast cancer]. I was by myself when he did. I thought about my kids and how I was going to take care of them. I had my surgery on March 23, 1988, and was home for my birthday on April first.

[Ingred has been divorced for ten years, so she had no husband to help her or to support her. She did have a boyfriend after the surgery, but she felt depressed and self-conscious about making love so she broke off the relationship.] "He was alright, but I wasn't."

[She continues to go for mammograms every year. Her oldest son at nineteen and her daughter helped her the most while she was going through the survival process. She didn't have chemo. Her hope is that her own daughters and sisters go for check ups. Her greatest fear is that the cancer will recur. During her treatment, Ingred prayed a lot. She prayed the Lord's prayer.] For other Native women I would tell them, not to get depressed and to get in a group. I was so depressed about it. [She seems depressed even now.]

Interview Analysis

In the native tradition of respecting a "guest in the house," Ingred was pleasant, polite, but guarded. Her interview was very short, only thirty minutes, answering my questions in monosyllabic monotones.

I understood her hesitancies and moved forward in the chair to show I cared about what she was telling me. I asked her if she could tell me more about [a certain] part of her life. She shook her head no. Reaching to hold her hand, I continued: "It must be very hard for you to tell a complete stranger these very personal things." She agreed that was true and quickly withdrew her hand.

"Why did you agree to the interview?" I asked finally.

"I want to help other women. And Claudette told me that it would be good to talk to you."

"Was it?" I asked.

She said, flatly, "It was OK."

In spite of my relaxation strategies, it was challenging for her to elaborate on her story. Perhaps she was ashamed of her poverty, or she was afraid that she would say the wrong thing. In some way, too, it seemed that Ingred feels her life isn't important and what she had been through as an abused woman and breast cancer survivor doesn't amount to much. Despite all she had overcome, perhaps because of it, her self-image has suffered. Is the mild depression she seems to be in constant? When I told her that the interview was over, she said, quite abruptly, "Good," as if she wished I had never come. I told her that her story is important to me, and I was appreciative of giving me her time for the interview. I also reiterated that it must be very hard for her to speak with me, considering that I was a stranger who just walked into her house and began asking such personal questions. She agreed, again, that this was true. Perhaps, even with my interviewing skills, I should have focused more on her skill as a beader or a speaker of her native language instead of my agenda? I am still learning to hear. Ingred is another breast cancer survivor from the north who has undergone sorrow and tragedy. She has much to share with other women. Her passiveness, too, was telling. Perhaps in needing to gain control of more of her life, she found the interview with me quite within her powers. She would allow me into her life story only so far and then, through her passiveness, no farther.

Baby: 1994

Baby, a contemporary twentieth-century woman, was raised as a foster child among the Aleut's by a White school teacher and her family. She speaks proudly of her foster mother, an amateur archeologist whose finds are in a number of museums in the Aleutian Islands of Alaska. One of her mother's displays and artifacts opened recently in an Aleutian museum.

After the interview, Baby agrees to have dinner with me, choosing a local Chinese restaurant called *HOW HOW,* located on the busy highway leading to Eagle River. Baby is triumphant about her struggle against alcoholism in her life. Her tidy ranch style home is newly decorated with paint and wallpaper which her family and friends helped to decorate, and she reflects on her Athabascan culture through her crafts and decoration for her home. "I never thought I would ever own my own place," she says, glancing around.

Again, as with most of the women in Alaska, I experience a sense of interacting with high school friends, although life for Baby has been more challenging and demanding than mine.

Baby's Story

Although I am Athabascan, I was raised along the Aleutian Islands. My [foster] mother was a school teacher. I was raised by foster parents. I have one foster brother and sister. My [foster] Dad was a carpenter for the BIA [Bureau of Indian Affairs].

We were living out with the Aleut. I can speak some Aleut words better than my own language. My mom never taught us the traditional skills

[she was a White schoolteacher hired by the BIA]. My mom taught a lot
of classes in a one-room school house. She was the teacher for my sister
and I all the way up to sixth grade! We had a bunch of kids in that
school, nineteen, but when I went to Kenai, we had over three hundred
and it was quite a difference.

There were sixty people in the village where we lived. It is almost to
the end of the Aleutian Islands, "McColesky" [on the island of
Chichagof]. We used to go fishing; we lived right by the ocean. Mostly
we ate sea food, sea urchins. We ate salmonberries, blueberries, halibut,
salmon; we also had seal, but I didn't like it. The government brought
sheep and cows to Chichagof. There was no hospital or nothing there.

My mom dug artifacts and some of them are in the museum in Kenai
now. My dad built our home in Kenai where I went to high school and
junior high. When I finished school, I went up to Anchorage in 1969
and I've been up here ever since. We went down when my mom was
here. She is eighty-four-years-old now. It's been eighteen years since
she's been up here. When we went down to Kenai, mom didn't recognize
anything; down there. I remember in '67–'68 they were going to build a
bridge and a subdivision. When we went there, it was all done. The only
thing I recognized was the inlet. Now there are subdivisions all the way
to Homer. When I was a kid, there was just a dirt road.

I went to Anchorage [after high school when she was eighteen years
old] because that's where the action is . . . more people . . . more everything. I got a job right off as a waitress in the club.

I was eleven when I had my first period and it was my mom who told
me about it. She told me, but they didn't speak very much about it because it was the fifties. She told me real briefly . . . and not to be mess-
ing up with boys. In the village it was taboo [to talk about it].

[Baby discussed her first period when she and her mother lived in the
Aleut villages. The Aleut have a different taboo on the first menses and
Baby was not at liberty to discuss with the other members of the village
that she had her first bleeding since she was not Aleut.] The following is
a description of the Aleut woman's first menses experience.

Then, in the custom of her people, her mother helped her make a
shelter of driftwood, mud, and grass. The girl stayed in there for
thirty days, eating little, using her dreams as ideas for designs [of
belts]. Hunters knew a woman in her first bleeding had special
powers, and any man who brought [the girl's] father seal skins had

the right to ask [the girl] to make a belt for him, something to give good fortune on hunting.

The hut had no walls, only a peaked roof of driftwood and grass mats that slanted down to the ground and was staked to the earth with bone pegs and kelp twine . . . the girl had not been allowed to help, only to watch, to wait in the darkness while her mother gathered grasses and driftwood and bought mats from their *ulaq*.* (Harrison, 1993, pp. 22–23)

I didn't want to have breasts. I was a real tomboy. She [her mother] tried to put me in a bra and I tied a strap around it. I was married in Kenai at sixteen and that lasted three years and then I got married again and was divorced fifteen years. I have a daughter who is twenty-eight and one that is fourteen. I breast fed the first one, but not the second one, because I was still drinking and I didn't want to breast feed her. My real mother died when she was twenty years old in Sitka, Mt. Edgecombe, of tuberculosis, in 1974. I'm from Tanacross [her Athabascan family roots] 100 miles from the Canadian border and my husband is from Northway 50 miles away from the Canada border. We used to go down there and party and we were out in the outhouse one time sitting on the two stools. A lady in the out house was sittin' there and she asked me where I was from. When she found out, she got all excited; she pulled up her britches and ran into the house shouting, "I found her, I found her."

Welfare pulled me out of the village [and put her in foster care] but they were trying to trace me for the Land Claims and my family had adopted me out [of the village]. My people and the elderly people told them that, "We adopted her out." I knew nothin' about my village or my relatives or my family until my second husband took me to Tanacross. All these cousins, uncles, and aunts started calling me up. My second husband said, "What if I am your cousin since my village is only 50 miles away. You might be my sister." I told him that I'd divorce him!

My dad [stepfather] died of leukemia at Elmendorf Air Base right after the earthquake [1964]. He was sixty-three. And my mom raised all of us by herself. My first husband was a GI because you're not "in" until you have a GI boyfriend. My second husband was Athabascan.

---

*Ulaq: communal house

I don't know if any other people in my family ever had cancer. [Baby found her own tumor while she was at home taking a shower. There was a lump near her nipple. She describes it as being smaller than a pencil eraser. Baby made an appointment right away to have herself examined. During the examination, she described how the lump was "sticking out." Several doctors examined her and the initial doctor told her that it was breast cancer without even doing a biopsy. They took out the lump under local anesthesia.]

I didn't even like it when he did that [the lumpectomy]. It [the tumor] looked like a piece of gristle; then he said "You don't have anything to worry about." A week or two later, I was at home in the shower gettin' ready for a date and the phone rings and here it was the doctor again. He told me over the phone, "You have malignant breast cancer." It was as if he was talking about the weather. It wasn't the same doctor [who did the lumpectomy]. He was talking to me as if I was stupid, "Do you know what cancer is?" [Baby worked in medical records and is very familiar and educated concerning all phases of medical terminology.] He told me over the phone that they were going to remove my breast. I told him, "NO, you are not going to remove my breast." He said, "From a surgeon's point of view that breast has to come off." I was mad at him. I told him, "I'm telling you from a patient's point of view, it isn't! You do it my way first and, if I'm dying, then you can take the breast off." I went in the bathroom and I started crying. I started praying. I asked God to "please let me live long enough to raise my one child that I waited so long to have. After that, you can do what ever you want with me." I was in a state of denial. I told Claudette [Amadon, head nurse, Outpatient Oncology Department of Alaska Native Medical Center], "I'll take chemotherapy, but I am totally angry about the whole situation." I was doing this as a precautionary manner, but I know that I don't have cancer. After they took the lump out, a couple of weeks later, they took the lymph nodes out and one was positive. The doctor wanted me to have the whole breast off. I also went through radiation after the lumpectomy. I had seven weeks of radiation, but I missed over half of it because of my alcoholism. I was either too drunk to go in or too sick to go in. The doctor actually called me and begged me to come in. He told me that I was too young to die. I did not like laying down and hated to be tied down. If they didn't tie me down, I would have been better. It happens to other people. When you read about it, you never think that it will happen to you. I had the best doctor in

Alaska [for radiation]. He also told me that I should have that breast removed. Someone came in and told me while I was laying on the [X-ray] table that if anything had gone wrong, I could be killed right there on the machine. If I had been killed on the [X-ray] machine, I wouldn't have to be tied down or go through radiation or chemotherapy, I'd be dead and take the short cut out. My mom said, "You don't say things like that." I went through a lot of anger. I wouldn't show any emotions, except for one time: I was strapped down and everyone was looking at me [on the X-ray machine] through the big iron door it was like a freak movie and I started crying and crying. One time I mixed sleeping pills with alcohol and banged into a door. Because of the bruises, I didn't go to X-ray that week. But I still have both my breasts.

During chemo, they told me all the detailed procedures and that they take blood tests every week. Because I didn't want it [the chemo], I proceeded to drink myself crazy the night before so that I would make my blood bad! The American Cancer Society had taxi drivers take me to therapy radiation and chemo. I lost a lot of hair, but I never had to wear a wig. I felt that I was going to make it. My landlord also helped me. She was a big Black lady and she took me to therapy and made me stay. She walked me right in there. She was a good Christian lady. My oldest girl also helped me and brought me to treatments. Welfare wanted to take my child, but I fought that. That also happened before when I was an alcoholic. I didn't want anyone touching my child or cleaning my house.

My friends and oldest daughter helped me the most. I was so angry. I was throwing tantrums and home alone with my little girl. I went into my bedroom, locked the door, and wanted to feel so sorry for Baby. There were so many times when I felt like giving up. My faith also helped me. I learned to have faith and it was a total miracle that I was cured of breast cancer and alcoholism. I read the literature that they gave me and recognized that I was in depression. I was angry at the people who were trying to help me. The fear of the unknown is worse than the diagnosis.

[Baby tells of a time when she played a trick on her sister. She was drinking with her girlfriend. She put on the wig and started crying that she lost all her hair and that she was a little bald girl. Her sister was shocked and then Baby pulled off the wig and started laughing and laughing.]

Interview Analysis

Baby has a boyfriend who doesn't smoke, drink, or take drugs. She goes to AA meetings now and likes her job. She feels that she is pretty happy. She never dreamed that she would ever own her own home.

Her main advice to other women is simple: "Get in to get examined as soon as possible. Read the literature; know about your emotions; join a group; know your rights. If you are fearful or angry, talk about it. Try not to run. Listen to doctor's advice."

Although Baby initially denied her breast cancer and refused to follow her physician's advice, she definitely wanted to be in control of her own treatment. Unfortunately, she took control by escaping into alcohol and denial. I am shocked at how her diagnosis was revealed. It is inconceivable that a physician would tell a woman that she had breast cancer over the phone! Such behaviors on the part of health care providers will be discussed further in the following chapter.

Today, however, Baby's obvious pride in what she was able to accomplish is exemplary and she is radiant in her joy of living.

ALASKA SUMMARY

In this chapter, I briefly discussed my initial impressions concerning the women in Anchorage. As I have said before, in Anchorage more treatment options were offered to Native women who experienced breast cancer than in other areas. For those who needed group support, more opportunities for women to participate in post-surgery support groups were available. In many ways, Anchorage is a typical American city offering such urban amenities as McDonald's, major grocery chains, and so on. At the same time, it also offers the negative aspects of urban life that those of us who live in the lower forty eight know so well: homelessness, substance abuse, problems resulting from population density. Yet Anchorage is also unique, and in many ways retains its unique cultural flavor—a vegetable soup of Alaska Natives, sourdough* history, settlers, and tourists.

---

*Sourdoughs: the name given to the gold miners of 1849 because they lived on sourdough bread.

For the Alaska Native people with ¹⁄₃₂ parts native blood line, Alaska Native Hospital will provide free treatment under the Indian Health Service. These and other issues are discussed further in the following chapter. I also touch on barriers to mammography access for women who live in remote villages of Alaska.

Silent Voices/Silent Stories

In the summer of 1995, I worked on the North Slope as a field assistant for the Institute of Arctic and Alpine Studies, University of Colorado. Thinking that my work would take me to Barrow so I could interview two Inupiat women who agreed to participate in the study, much to my consternation, this did not materialize. I hesitated to interview them by phone because I wanted face-to-face oral histories in the traditional way. One day, I hope to bring their voices to our table of stories.

According to Ian Gilchrist, Chief Medical Officer for the Northwest Territories, there are six breast cancer survivors scattered about in remote villages in the Northwest Territories of Canada. Because of stringent limitations put on researchers by the Provincial Government and the Inuit people in the Northwest Territories, and my lack of funding, I could not interview these women as part of this study. But this group of women deserves to be heard. I hope to be their voice—one day.

Transcultural Health Care: The Cry

Native women have access to Indian Health Service Care and native health care. Repeatedly Eurocentric in approach, IHS Care is often given in ignorance and with little respect to the individual woman or her culture. Frequently, too, the deleterious effects of the medicine coupled with the sometimes abusive care overshadows any admirable care that is given. For their part, non-native women who are poor, rural or urban, also face a cancer diagnosis and possible death without proper medical access even today. For both native and non-native women that fact drives fear and isolation into rage, deeper depression, resulting in more victimization and fewer survivors. Clearly, too, as indigenous cultures continue moving forward on a path with technology and progress, they may gain more convenient lifestyles, but at a cost: loss of cultural values and damage to the environment. To protect what is theirs culturally, many tribes have begun compacting* with the federal government to staff Indian Health Service facilities with Indian nurses and physicians who are sensitive of and responsive to cultural identities and variances. As a result, not only are there certain economic savings for the federal government, but health care is delivered by each tribe in a new tribal health environment that promotes respect of native cultures.

---

*Compacting with the federal government: The self-governance process can promote tribal sovereignty, improve health care, maximize tribal involvement in developing and managing programs, and enhance relationships between health care workers and the population served. To give American Indians and Alaska Natives more independence and power related to the implementation of federal mandates, in amendments PL93-638 section 302 and 307, Congress required the Health and Human Services Secretaries and the Secretary of the Interior to conduct a research demonstration project. Thirty tribes were selected to participate and to negotiate annually to enter into funding agreements to take over the planning and delivery of some or all of federal services. Final budgets are federally funded with overages to be carried by the tribes themselves. (*Indian Health Service Provider*, October, 1995.)

Churchill, Manitoba—Traditional Inuit Hide tanning. Photo by the author.

Chapter 5

CELEBRATING THE CIRCLE OF KNOWING

Journal: 4/9/95 Spring has arrived in Montana. Days are longer. Although the snow on the peaks of the Mission Mountains will linger until July, the valley is warm. Silent, snowy fields have yielded to voices of meadowlarks, robins, and territorial songs of nesting red-winged black birds. In greening pastures, wobbly February calves, now a bit stronger and surer of their steps, frolic with their mothers. Wintering eagles and visiting tundra swans, their sexual drive urging them on, have abandoned us for their northern nesting grounds. In the mountains, hibernating bears are awakening. Another circle of life begins.

My mother's breast cancer is in remission. Her recent bone and liver scans indicate a cancer-free body. The news gives us cause to celebrate. No longer is my mother afraid that she is dying. Her skeletal pains of last winter have been diagnosed as arthritis. Her mind is clear and free of alcohol when I call her. We plan a visit in May—she is happy, eager for me to come. She talks of a trip to Montana this Fall. I celebrate her presence in the "circle of knowing."

Belenkey's research (1986) tells us that, as women, our pathways to knowledge are many. We listen to the voices of others. Our knowledge develops from separate yet connected knowledge, stories from intuition and instinct. From these sources we construct layers of meaning which evolve with each new experience and shared story. In this chapter, I celebrate and illustrate the circle of knowing of shared knowledge gained from Northern Native Women's breast cancer stories. In this journey, I too have gained knowledge (Belenkey, 1986). As women, the informants and I share a common unity approaching, as Peck (1987) has put it, a veritable concept of community: ". . . where everyone is safe. It is a safe place to be angry; a safe place to let our guard down; a safe place to be us. A circle has no sides in our community. As members of the community we are committed to one another; to hang in there for one another no matter how tough it gets; we are committed." Through the sharing of stories, Northern Native Women and I have created community whose center is lit with a "knowing" fire, the women ringed round in a circle with no sides.

In listening to the experienced voices of my elders, grandmothers, and sisters, I hear their concerns of health and self-determination reflected in my own mirror. The women's voices are authoritative, lively, and self-respectful, and clear in contrast to the coolly analytical voices of scientists or medical care providers. Whether the women are Northern Native Women or Caucasian women living in the lower forty-eight states, their reactions to breast cancer share many commonalities, such as fear, hope, resignation, and more.

In addition to documenting the stories of women in Alaska and Labrador who were diagnosed with breast cancer, I have also documented my thoughts and feelings, a process which feminist scholars call reflexivity (see Appendix C). This process gave me insight into my own life's journey and uncovered commonalities between my own experiences and those of the women I interviewed (Fonow & Cook, 1991).

Circle of life legends are told by a number of Native American tribes through a variety of stories. In their worldview, Navajo People tell the legend of Changing Woman, a symbol of earth who represents the cyclic path of the seasons: birth, spring; maturing, summer; growing old, fall; and dying, winter. The stories of Native Northern Women bear witness to the changes that breast cancer causes in the circle of their own lives; changes that involve their mental, emotional, spiritual, and cultural energies. These changing circles are discussed next.

THE NURTURING WOMAN IMAGE

Not only are breasts important to nourish newborn life, breasts are a hall-mark of a complete woman and a completely sexual woman. As the litera-ture on Caucasian women who have undergone mastectomy notes, a sense of fear, isolation, powerlessness, lost womanness, and suicidal thoughts often accompany the loss of a breast (Rollins, 1976; Wadler, 1992; Williamson, 1993). In the stories told here, Native Northern Women also value breasts as a life giver and as a symbol of womanhood. When breasts are stricken with cancer, the values and symbols associated with them can also suffer. Yet the negative emotions and thoughts that can then arise can be salved by support and nurturing from a circle of family, friends, and community. The positive attitudes such support engenders coupled with a return to tradi-tional cultural pursuits can also provide balance, a balance sometimes des-perately needed, and give Northern Native Women strength in healing.

Rejected Woman Images

On that day, something more than cold hung in the air as The People gathered around their few flickering fires and listened to the chief. . . . He spoke about the cold, hard days they were to expect if they were to survive the winter. . . . Then he announced in a clear loud voice: "We are going to leave the old women behind." The women were stunned as a sense of shock overcame them. Though they wanted to cry out, no words came. They felt as if they were in a terrible nightmare. (Wallis, 1993)

—Athabascan Legend

Prior to European contact, Arctic women were valued for their sur-vival skills rather than for their appearance (Billson, 1988). Today, North-ern cultures have blended and clashed with other cultures and many alien values have held sway. Today, breasts, not skills, are associated with being a woman.

The shock of being diagnosed with breast cancer and concern about getting appropriate surgery may be just the beginning of a woman's wor-ries (Schover, 1991). Women with breast cancer can feel terribly isolated, and not only from those close to them, but from all other women with healthy breasts. Being alone when told of the diagnosis may also increase fears of rejection. Caucasian women in North America have expressed their feelings this way: "We must come to terms with our own mortality and master fear, despair, loneliness, grief and rage. The medical establishment, too, enters into this expression, 'Women are [then] catapulted into dangerous and unfamiliar territory dealing with doctors, nurses, testing and medical terminology'" (Kaye, 1991, p. 33).

When faced with a diagnosis of breast cancer, the Northern Native Women interviewed in this study experienced emotions similar to their Caucasian neighbors: rejection, loneliness from social isolation, and fear of dying. Rubra, married for just six months when she discovered her breast cancer, expressed her feelings of rejection this way, "I told him [her husband] to find a more whole woman, but he loved me and stayed with me." Rubra, knowing that his first wife had also died of breast cancer, did not want him to go through this again with her. But he loved her, gave her support, and encouraged her. As she finally put it, "Sometimes I have an image of myself as half a woman, but that there is no one in the world like me."

In Anchorage, Baby's fear of rejection, magnified by a history of personal difficulties, were even more pronounced. As a means to escape possible disfigurement and possible death, she drank and smoked marijuana excessively.

Joan's experience and view of herself were tied intimately to her life with her husband. "He's wonderful," Joan explained. "I don't know how he puts up with all of it." Joan never did explain what "all of it" meant, but by the concerned look on her face I interpreted this to mean: "I am fearful of rejection by the sight of my breastlessness when we make love for the first time. We haven't made love yet since the second mastectomy. My body has gone through so much and the desire isn't there, yet." Joan also told me that Claudette Amadon has a teaching video for couples whose partners have gone through mastectomy. "We [Joan and husband] are going to watch it together," she concluded.

For her part, Fiona told me that her husband was "OK" but that she "felt like half a woman." When she and her husband made love for the first time after the mastectomy, it was Fiona who suggested, quite impishly, that he "suck my false tittie." [But he didn't.]

Stories from the women in Labrador are similar. Sally revealed that her husband was "OK with it [the loss of her breast]. I guess that there were some feelings there, but he didn't show them." When I interviewed her,

Sally hadn't yet looked at her "ugly" scar. Sally is dealing with feelings of rejection because of her perceived disfigurement. Do those fears ever go away? Mimi also told me that her husband was ". . . glad that I didn't die, eh, and he loves me anyway." Lilly had few problems with her husband's feelings since he had prostate cancer and was going through his own loss.

Among the Labradorian Native Women whom I interviewed, images of isolation and rejection were exacerbated by illiteracy and cultural deprivation. Of the four Native Women in the study who live in Labrador, each was told her diagnosis when she was alone and away from her village undergoing treatment in St. John's, Newfoundland. Because each woman was isolated from her family, relatives, friends and support systems, each women suffered a more poignant sense of rejection for having no person nearby she knew and trusted with whom to discuss her fears and feelings.

Mimi, unable to read or write, was even more isolated because she was unable to write home. Ellen, who was quite literate, was equally isolated because of her husband's illiteracy—and his inability to respond to the letters she sent home. Ellen was also isolated by language. She yearned for an interpreter who could speak her own language of Inuktitut to her.

Cultural isolation was also a factor for Native women to contend with. Two of the women focused on the food given to them in the hospital. Although admitting that the hospital food was nutritious, still it was "different" from their country foods. Mimi mentioned that the food was good, but decidedly different. Ellen noted that the food was "not the same" as what she was used to eating. All of the Native Labradorian Women expressed anxiety concerning care for their families while they were undergoing treatment. And, as mentioned previously, the women desired to have the physical and emotional support of a husband, partner, or relative when told of their diagnosis of breast cancer. Because of the closeness of the family unit, native or otherwise, it is critical that *all* women have someone there to give emotional support when first told about the cancer. Women deserve that right; they should not be without emotional support in the face of such an emotional crisis. Yet that is exactly the position Northern Native Women face particularly when they are removed from their villages to larger hospitals for diagnosis and treatment. As Betty Rollins (1976) stated so succinctly, "First you cry." We need companions to cry with us.

Although the women I interviewed may have felt rejected and isolated, and many of the men unable to discuss their woman's breast cancer openly, it was heartening to discover the emotional support, the love and partnership, that Northern Native Men gave to their Women. The men, whether actively or passively, accepted their role as silent, loving guardian. They stood by through chemotherapy, vomiting, hair loss, depression, and continued to love their wives and care for them. It would be an enlightening study to gather information on the role of partners and men in breast cancer healing. As one husband not connected to the present study put it: "To say I would not want my wife's breast back would be a lie. I wish I could wave my hand and undo all that has happened . . . I miss them, but not enough to get carried away with it" (Murcia & Stewart, 1989, p. 117). Carter, a Caucasian woman, tells us, "Bless the husbands and lovers who kiss our bald heads and tell us we look beautiful, and sit next to us during our chemo sessions making us laugh. Bless the ones who have assumed a partnership role in the whole ordeal" (1993).

Personal Reflection

When my dad learned that mom was planning breast reconstruction, he was horrified that she willingly sought out another surgical procedure. "Don't do this for me," he said. But my mother was adamant. "I want to look good in clothes," she insisted. "I want to do this for myself." And she did. She took a risk when the procedure for breast reconstruction was in its infancy. She did it to add a semblance of control over the events in her life. She did it to increase her self-esteem. She did it to improve her self-image and reduce her fears of isolation. She refused to feel rejected because she had no breasts.

Lost Woman Images

The women [who have been rejected by their clan] walked late into the night . . . They stumbled numbly on, many times falling in the snow from sheer fatigue and old age. Yet, they pushed on, almost in desperation, knowing that each step brought them closer to their destination. . . . Sometimes fatigue clouded their judgment, and they found themselves straying off course or going in circles . . . . (Wallis, 1993)

—Athabascan Legend

Following the loss of their breasts, the Native Northern Women I interviewed reported feelings of being half a woman, of being a woman lost to themselves and to those near them. This sense of loss appeared even more prevalent in the women from Alaska, where dominant Western cultural values—from the lower forty-eight—and which emphasize the sexual importance of breasts for women, overshadow traditional native values of women being important for their skills. Three Alaskan women I interviewed were depressed enough to use alcohol and marijuana as escape mechanisms. Rubra, Baby, and Fiona all admitted to "bringing" on alcohol and pot as a means of escape. Rubra ". . . went on a binge for a week before her surgery." Baby reported that she was ". . . always too drunk to go to chemo. If I make my blood bad, they won't give it to me." Fiona and Rubra also used marijuana as a therapeutic means of tempering the effects of chemotherapy, which caused them to vomit, lose hair, and develop candidiasis of the mouth.

The sense of being a lost woman was especially prevalent for Labradorian women. However, this was partially due to the fact that their husbands, when compared to Anchorage husbands, found it more difficult to talk of the woman's loss. In Inuit culture, whether for good or ill, women problems are a "woman's business" and not "a hunter's business." Because of such ingrained attitudes, Labradorian women had really no one with whom to share their feelings of loss. Metzger (1981) depicts poignantly the feeling of loss: "She cries every morning when she gets dressed. She looks for gathered blouses, bodices, and tunics which will not display or thrust her loss too visibly in the stranger's eye or in the eye of the friend." Lilly echoes such feelings in her own statement, "I could find no dresses to wear."

Winter Woman Images

. . . (T)he blue this time of winter meant cold. Soon it would be colder as night approached. . . . We can sit here and wait to die. We would not have long to wait . . . if we are going to die, my friend, let us die trying, not sitting. (Wallis, 1993)

—*Athabascan Legend*

Northern Native Women who have had breast cancer expressed feelings of depression and imminent death, which I call winter woman images. Their depression stems from fear of surgery, chemotherapy, the unknown, and fear of death. Two women in Labrador, Lilly and Mimi, even felt suicidal. When faced with the prospect of the devastating effect that their suicide would have on their families, however, their hope of escape by suicide faded, and thankfully so. But their depression continued. As Lilly said, "I felt just like jumping out of that door there, but I wouldn't do it." Ellen expressed her more general fears of death in this way: "I got all these kids and a husband, and I'm gonna die of cancer." Mimi was definite in her expectations of dying. "Just give me two more years 'til my kids get bigger," she said.

Two women in Anchorage also reported feeling suicidal. But they, like Lilly and Mimi, responded more to the love and support their families gave them and needed in return. Joan told me, "I didn't really feel like killing myself. I wouldn't do that to my family, but when you are going through all of the treatments, you wish that you would hurry and get better or quietly fade away."

In Anchorage Baby said, "I was told over the telephone. The doctor said, 'Do you know how sick you are? Do you know you could die?'" Ingred was also alone when told of her diagnosis, which increased her sense of isolation and rejection. She expressed her concern about her imminent death by speaking of her children: "I got no one to care for my kids."

Women who have been diagnosed with breast cancer have a good reason to be depressed. From the time of their diagnosis they lose control of their own lives, they are alienated from their culture, and their self-image is undermined.

> The words, "I am dying," hum through my head endlessly and without relief. I hear that melody all the time. . . . What can I write about that aloneness? . . . You cannot know the aloneness of one who faces death, looking at it squarely in the eye. (Butler & Rosenblum, 1991, p. 119)

Healing Woman Images: The Medicine Wheel

For all the people of the earth, the Creator has given us the medicine wheel to guide us in our pathways. It is an ancient and powerful symbol of the universe. Like a mirror, the medicine wheel helps us to see what is past, what is present, and what is future. It helps us to understand things we cannot see because they are ideas and not physical objects. (Bopp, J. et al., 1984)

The medicine wheel teaches us that we have four aspects to our nature: the physical, the mental, the emotional, and the spiritual. Each of these aspects must be equally developed in a healthy, well-balanced individual. To find balance and healing according to the natural order, we must seek the center of the Medicine Wheel where all aspects are in balance. In seeking the center of the Medicine Wheel, we experience adaptation—a process in which an organism changes its genetic structure or changes a behavior in response to stimuli in the environment. Genetic change can be a lengthy process that develops over generations while behavioral change is often an immediate behavioral response to a stimulus. In nursing assessment, adaptation refers to the client's response to healing as a result of nursing interventions. By using a variety of survival strategies in seeking

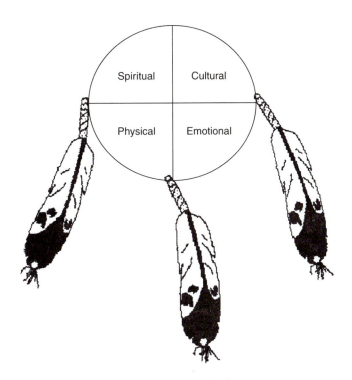

The Medicine Wheel

the balanced center of the Medicine Wheel, the Native Northern Women I interviewed have adapted to breast cancer and are healing. Like the two old women in the Athabascan legend, they have survived by utilizing skills and strategies valued by their culture.

. . . Many days went by before the women caught more rabbits. . . . They managed to preserve their energy by boiling spruce boughs to serve as a minty tea, but it made the stomach sour. . . . [T]he two women first boiled the rabbit meat to make a nourishing broth, which they drank slowly. . . . The hunting skills that they learned in their youth re-emerged. (Wallis, 1993)

—*Athabascan Legend*

Cultural Practices in the Circle of Healing

"When people become frustrated and disillusioned, they often turn to rituals and mechanisms to regain a sense of control, to revitalize their culture and to restore equilibrium. In reaffirming ethnic identity, these movements reduce the psychological stress of rapid change" (McElroy & Townsend, 1985). For many of the women interviewed, connection to their Native culture has increased their awareness of who they are and has aided in their breast cancer healing. Traditional foods, free of chemicals and processing, are used as a significant remedy here.

In Anchorage, for instance, Fiona ate fish soup, as her forebears had, after her breast surgery, including eating the eyes to aid her in healing. Fiona also used seal oil to soothe the irritation of her breast skin lesions. Seal oil was an important part of grooming her hair and mouth during chemotherapy as well. She said, "See my hair, no grey since the chemo and my skin, no wrinkles. I look good! It is because of the seal oil." Joan, on the other hand, who was less attracted to traditional unguents, couldn't ". . . stand the smell of seal oil." However, she did admit that her mother is ". . . big on seals." For her part, Glenda purchased organic products from her local health food store.

Since her breast cancer diagnosis, Rubra has gained strength from her Haida traditions. She has turned to making traditional red and black blankets with white buttons outlining the shape of Eagle, Orca, and Raven. She engages in craft-making and listening to traditional music. She speaks with pride of the women in Hydaburg who are continuing the traditions. Rubra also eats only Sunrider foods, which are free of chemicals.

Maxine turned to her embroidery for healing. Embroidering a quilt for her son gave her much pleasure during recovery. Although she did not articulate these thoughts, it is understood by Maxine and her son that the quilt will live beyond her, giving her son something to remember her by.

In Labrador, Ellen used the healing properties of Labrador tea (Ledum), a local herb, to help her dry throat after cobalt therapy. Ellen also eats pure "country foods" such as caribou and seal for protein. She complained that the food ". . . in the stores from the south are full of chemicals." Ellen also busies herself with traditional crafts, such as working with buckskin in the sewing of miniature moccasins.

In Anchorage, during Joan's three-hour interview, she continually stressed the importance of hope and positive attitude. She tells me that it is hard to keep a positive attitude because this is the second time that she has had breast cancer, and this time the metastisis is more aggressive. She knows that her positive attitude is ". . . so important for her family's sake."

Rubra's positive attitude has helped her to decide that she will be able to overcome breast cancer. She told me pointedly, "I have it because I am strong enough to get over it. No one else in my family would be like me [in fighting it]."

Maxine turned to religion and her spirituality to develop her positive attitude. When she was admitted to the hospital for a second brain metastasis, she used prayer to help her pull through. Her husband and sons also surrounded her with love as did everyone in the community. She never spoke of feeling isolated or rejected. Her post mastectomy feelings were those of a strong woman in love with life.

A sense of humor also helped the women I interviewed keep balance in a depressing world of drugs, surgery, and chemotherapy. Joan's playful removing her wig after the interview caught me off guard somewhat. "Bet you'd like to get that on TV," she said, laughing, referring to her bald head. Then there was Fiona asking her husband to ". . . suck her false tittie" and Baby, who put on her wig and cried to her sister that "she was a bald little girl" when, in fact, she was playing a joke. Mimi, in Labrador, jokingly wanted to have a T-shirt made which read, "Dr. Fitz fixed my tits."

To help in her healing, Ellen from Labrador would have liked to have had a support group to attend when she went home from the hospital in Newfoundland. "It would be better than gossiping all of the day," she concluded. But Ellen is certainly not alone here. One option for Ellen as other isolated women would be a conference call initiated at the nurses' clinic once or twice a month to link a group of women with the same diagnosis who could then share experiences. In many rural areas, much is being done with distance learning and telemedicine.

Women helping women by means of support groups was an important factor in many recovery stories. Every one of the women in Labrador and in Alaska went to a support group meeting at least once. Although Glenda told me that she preferred to ". . . get well my way by going to the gym and taking special diets," the majority of women thought that attending support groups was helpful.

Support groups are available to the Labradorian women I interviewed, but only during their stay in the hospital for treatment. The lack of support groups in their villages added to these women's sense of isolation when they returned home. Women in northern Canada seem to suffer more from cultural and social isolation as a result of having to leave their culture and their village for diagnosis, surgery, and treatment. Unfortunately, it is impossible from this study to determine how such isolation affects the rate and quality of their healing.

Community and family support is another key to healing. In Hydaburg, Alaska, friends in the community banded together to raise money through cake sales, dances, and car washes for Rubra and Linda to travel to Greece for experimental treatments. Their communities supported them personally and supported their choice of experimental treatment methods for breast cancer.

I spoke by phone to a sixty-seven-year-old breast cancer survivor, an Inuk from Iqaluit who had agreed to be interviewed, but her life was so busy gathering berries, caring for grandchildren, attending the elders meetings, and digging clams that we never could find a time or location for the interview. Her surgery took place in her own city of Iqaluit where there were many bilingual Inuit to interpret the English words spoken by the Canadian physicians. Her family was there to provide the emotional support she needed while she was in the hospital for surgery. Shouldn't this woman's experience be the norm for other native women?

OUR GRANDMOTHER'S TRAIL:
RETURNING TO NORMAL

What are women's lives like after suffering the horrific experience breast cancer? Can they return to the normality of their lives before cancer? The answer is complex for each woman. But each woman also knows that her body is not the same as it was. They are different physically as well as emotionally. Their immediate worlds can also change. Many employers, for instance, have discriminated against women with breast cancer. Insurance companies won't "take them on" as new buyers or pay for irregular or experimental treatments, or even reconstruction if it is wanted. Yet women *have* survived. They try to forget that they are one-breasted women or no-breasted women. As Fiona would say, "We wear our false titties."

Some women do go for reconstruction. With their scarred bodies they return to their work. They love, work out, cook meals, create special moments with family and friends. They "give back" to others, perhaps to be remembered, perhaps to forget, even momentarily, their loss. Still, they are strong. They help other women survive. They help their families survive. But can they ever forget the experiences that have made them breast cancer survivors?

Maxine is eager for school to start so that she can help other children through the Head Start Program in Anchorage. Glenda sought out physical exercise. Others, in joining support groups, have helped by sharing their stories with newly diagnosed women. Joan has opted to stay at home and reduce her workload, so that she can be a mother and help her five-year-old son. As part of her healing process, Rubra has worked helping her friends, selling Sunrider foods, as well as for building a cash economy in the community of Hydaburg. For Mimi, in Labrador, working the seal skins and creating beautiful crafted mukluk boots has helped her healing.

In the lower forty-eight states of America, women all over the country are speaking up about breast cancer. These women are on the forefront of a revolution. They are not able to wait quietly and passively for miracle cures, so they are bringing breast cancer directly into public awareness (Dowling & Fineman, 1994). Women in America are fighting back with interleukin, antigen vaccines, and STEM Cell and bone marrow replacement techniques. Phyllis Newman (1994), a broadway actress who survived breast cancer, gives us this message of hope: "I want to put out the message that life does go on. Following my second mastectomy in 1984, I took tamoxifen for two years. Since then I've been treatment free. I don't feel like I'm living under a cloud. Worrying about it doesn't prevent it. I just feel grateful and lucky."

Personal Reflection

My mother's positive attitude and sense of humor inspired and saved all of us from having to face our own terror and dread of the future. From her, we learned that there was life after breast cancer, a rich, full life. Her physicians marveled at her sense of humor. She was selected as a hospital volunteer, inspiring other women undergoing their own frightful experiences with breast cancer and the medical community.

Medicine Men and Images

"In the case of missionary contact with Northern people, one of the first tasks of the missionaries was to discredit the shaman.* The seizure of power from the shaman interrupted a traditional approach to holistic healing" (Minor, 1992). The system of healing and the use of specific healers emerges directly from the prevalent worldview of each culture. Most Western-oriented medical personnel believe that Western scientific medicine is superior to all other medical forms. And this may be true for particular treatments. However, medical practitioners in other cultures have been treating patients successfully for centuries (Galanti, 1990). Many of our modern drugs, such as quinine, have also been discovered in native medical kits [medicine bundles].

The late Eskimo healer, Della Keates, supposedly healed many patients through the use of touch, love, and a combination of old and new

---

*Among First Nations Peoples, medicine men and shamans are generally chosen by the gods, usually through a celestial sign such as lightning. Once chosen, their training is guided by an older shaman or medicine man or woman. In some Rocky Mountain tribes, the power of shamans and medicine is transferred to a child in the family through a dream. In other tribes, the power comes through visions and fasting. In a few cultures women could be shaman, but it is rare. "An Igulik became a shaman after being wounded by a walrus" (Eliade, 1964, p. 22). His mother was a shaman after a fireball entered her body (Eliade, 1964). As healers and medicine men/women, these holy people commune with animal and woodland spirits on behalf of others. They are respected today as sources of traditional wisdom.

medicines. The older Eskimo people also give credence to the power of touch as a direct result of the shaman's healing power (Geiger & David-hizar, 1991).

Although the women I interviewed denied using shamanistic powers or traditional folk medicine, I found that touch was an important compo-nent of communication, especially for the women in Labrador. During those interviews, we would hold hands, hug, or exchange touches. Because I was a newcomer into their lives, perhaps even if the women did use the shaman's power, they would not have shared that information with me. Either they did not use it, or they denied using it because they didn't trust me with that knowledge.

For their part, the Anchorage women were too far removed from their traditions to be in a position to use the shaman's power, although some may have practiced folk medicine. However, when I asked them about it, they denied it as well.

Among the adjuvant therapies for the nausea and vomiting associated with chemotherapy is marijuana. Derived from the Indian Hemp plant, Cannabis sativa, it has been approved by the Federal Drug Administration (FDA) in tablet or injection forms. The active ingredient in marijuana is tetrahydrocannabinol or THC. Although THC can even be given orally, pa-tients get better results from smoking it (Amadon, 1994). Perhaps by smok-ing, marijuana diffuses more quickly throughout the blood stream than by any other method aside from intravenous. The Federal Drug Association (FDA) has approved the tablets, but not alternative forms such as smoking pot. Fiona and Ruba both agreed that chemotherapy was more bearable after smoking pot.

WOMAN: FEARFUL AND COURAGEOUS

. . . [She] managed a slight smile . . . but continued to stare dully into the fire. "I sit and worry," she said after a long silence. "I fear what lies ahead." (Wallis, 1993)

—Athabascan Legend

Women who survive breast cancer live with many fears: fear of rejection, of isolation, of death, of not being a woman. These fears develop from the realization that they won't live long enough for their children to grow up, that they won't be able to grow old with their husbands, and that they no longer know or control their bodies. "Many women who have had breast cancer say they are fearful that the disease will recur. They become anxious about physical symptoms and ailments, interpreting every ache or pain as a signal that their cancer has returned" (Kaye, 1991, p. 65).

The women in the study told me that surviving breast cancer has made them stronger; they can face anything now. However, the greatest fear for all of the women is the fear of early death and the fear of cancer reoccurrence.

In Anchorage, Linda complained of abdominal pain and discomfort. She indicated that although the doctor told her she was under stress, she thinks the pain signals a return of her cancer. Other women like Glenda denied having any fears.

In Labrador, Ellen complained of recurring sore throat pain. I asked Ellen what she thought her sore throat might be from and she told me, ". . . my cancer coming back." Sally told me that she doesn't worry about it: "Let someone else worry," as she put it. But some women expressed fear that their cancers were recurring elsewhere in their bodies. Younger mothers wanted to see their children on their own, or graduated from high school. Mimi asked for "just two more years," so her kids would be bigger. Other women discussed the fact that their families would suffer untold sadness at their death. Maxine and Joan, with the disease in stage IV, its most dangerous phase, are especially aware of how their deaths would affect their families. Maxine said, "It would cause such sadness and loss to my husband and boys. It would be hard for them for the first two years. Then they [will] begin to remember the good times and healing for them will begin." Dissolving into tears, Joan told me, "[my greatest fear] is that I won't be there for my son to grow up and that my husband and I won't grow old together."

In counterpoint to their fears, the women also possessed great courage, with Rubra, Joan, Linda, and Baby demonstrating risk-taking behaviors. Recall Linda and Rubra traveling to Greece to undergo an experimental vitamin treatment of which they had little or no understanding. Joan, one of two Native Alaskans selected by the IHS to participate in a highly controversial and experimental STEM Cell* assay technique, left her home and family in Anchorage to begin the experiment in Seattle, Washington.

Joan's willingness to know and do as much as she could to combat the cancer was also clear when she told me that: "There is a better method of mammography now called MRI.[†] I wish that they had that for me." As a risk taker, Joan would have gladly traveled to Houston to have an MRI if the opportunity had presented itself.

Baby also found her voice as a risk taker. She braved the anger of the medical doctors in Anchorage and refused to have a mastectomy. Baby also fought against chemotherapy, but eventually went through the treatment because of her association with Claudette Amadon, head nurse of the chemotherapy unit at Alaska Native Hospital, who understands the culture and the women. Claudette was always spoken of as "a caring, gentle chemo nurse."

Of the women who knew about the treatment with Tamoxifen,[‡] however, only Maxine agreed to use it. Linda, a biochemist, was especially adamant about refusing to participate in the study.

In contrast, the Labradorian women in the study did not demonstrate risk-taking behaviors. They willingly agreed to the treatments offered to them by the medical system. They were not offered, nor did they research treatments other than mastectomy and cobalt therapy.

---

*STEM Cell: The STEM Cell method of treatment occurs at the interface of test tube research and clinical application. In this method of treatment, cancer cells are removed from the patient, cultured in flasks and different drugs tested on the samples to determine which drugs are effective. A drug which will not kill a cancer cell in a flask will usually not kill it in the patient. But an effective drug in a culture will also not necessarily be effective in the patient (Laszio, 1987, p. 291).

[†]The MRI or magnetic resonance imaging technique was developed at Baylor College of Medicine in Houston, Texas. MRI can detect growths as tiny as three millimeters by producing an image of the breast with radio waves and magnetic fields. Currently, in Houston, research is being carried out to develop an MRI needle and breast biopsy procedure.

[‡]Tamoxifen: A drug which blocks estrogen function and may prevent breast cancer. The National Cancer Institute (NCI) is exploring, through a seven-year study, whether tamoxifen actually blocks estrogen receptors and may be able to prevent breast cancer from occurring in high-risk women (Laszio, 1987). There are many adverse effects from tamoxifen, such as hot flashes, nausea, increased risk of blood clots, and liver tumors.

The Circle Game: Breast Cancer Politics

It is important to note that there is a politics of breast cancer survival and treatment. Political and social action groups, formed by women such as Women's Environment and Development Organization (WEDO), The Breast Cancer Coalition, and the Breast Cancer Fund direct their economic power to improve the state of women including Native women. Petitioning congress (uncapitalized by choice) for more research monies, more access to health care when it involves mammography and breast reconstruction, and more research on discovering the link between breast cancer and the environment has helped to increase funding for breast cancer research from $88 million in 1990 to $300 million in 1994. Today, breast cancer receives more funding than any other cancer. Yet many Native Women in the American and Canadian north as well as their governments have yet to recognize that we share an epidemic.

Healers, Wisdom, and White Man's Medicine

As used by French (1985), patriarchy is an ideology founded on the assumption that man is distinct from and superior to all creatures in the animal kingdom. Similarly, and to protect its status, patriarchy has caused the demise of women and women's rights, especially in traditional cultures. The treatment of women by the Jesuits who arrived in the New World bringing the "gift" of Christianity is a case in point, and one among many. Unfortunately, such treatment continues to hold sway today both in developing countries (Shiva, 1993) and in the United States. Patriarchy, which is epitomized in Western medical structures, and also known to indigenous peoples as White man's medicine, focuses on eradicating disease of which human beings are the incidental host. The values placed on the healing of a person or on respect of that person and her links to the natural world do not seem to be held with equal esteem.

> Health conditions among native populations, and the manner in which health care services are currently delivered in the North, reflect the colonial legacy that has profoundly influenced northern society. Along some dimensions of morbidity and mortality, indicators in northern native population rival, and in so many cases surpass, those of Third World countries. (Crnkovich, 1993, p. 82)

Feelings of powerlessness and isolation characterized the Northern Native breast cancer patients I interviewed, many of whom were unable to understand the medical terminology and procedures that their doctors in urban hospitals expected them to undergo. Other women, despite being fluent in the terminology, reported feeling powerless and degraded by paternalistic physicians.

Women in Labrador as well as in Anchorage complained that the physician did not offer options to the treatment prescribed. Women in Anchorage with a college or beyond high school degree were treated as if they were ignorant and knew nothing about breast cancer, as in the cases of Baby and Linda (who has a degree in biochemistry). The women also complained that physicians treated them in a disrespectful manner and were "always in a hurry." This behavior by physicians undermines the self-esteem of Native American Women.

American Indian and Alaskan Native People have a worldview, ethical values, and concerns for both the individual and the community that may differ from those of the medical establishment, and which may then contribute to misunderstanding. Although the Labradorian women had more positive things to say about their physicians than did the Alaskan women, for example, even they in large part expressed concern, especially over not understanding the medical terms health care workers used. They reported that the doctors didn't take sufficient time to explain things and they (the women) were too afraid to ask. Initially, the women felt isolated, afraid for their lives. Their diagnosis was a death sentence to them and they feared for themselves and for the families they would not be able to care for. Mimi's reaction, while somewhat extreme, is also revealing: she didn't want to go home at first because she thought that she would contaminate her family.

As health-care providers working with women from various cultures, we all need to take time to understand the culture of each patient. We must take time to explain procedures more fully and at the level of understanding of the patient. Health care providers also need to cultivate awareness and respect of the needs of elders, who are "Keepers of Earth Wisdom" in their native cultures. Until then, the achievement of health and healing for native women will be elusive. Fortunately, there are exceptions within the established White man's medicine practices.

Delivery of culturally appropriate health care in a pluralistic society demands that practitioners develop special attributes, knowledge, and skills. Here, the exploration of personal values is an essential first step in developing cultural awareness, to move beyond ethnocentrism, to adopt a multicultural approach to professional practice (Carpio & Mujundar, 1993, p. 4).

Even as recently as 1991, Leininger notes the absence of anthropological knowledge as a specific domain in educating medical students and nurses. Universities need to create an awareness of how culture influences health care (Larson, 1984). With increased transcultural knowledge and communication skills, health care providers will be able to provide meaningful, therapeutic care.

Several years ago as a young graduate nurse, I spent two years working in the Philippines. In the cities as well as in small barrios, non-Western, traditional health care practices were common. Women healers, for example, use a necklace of garlic bulbs around a baby's neck to protect it from the spells of witches. When a newly delivered mother returns home from the hospital, after being treated by Western medicine, the healer has her sit on a smudge pot of special healing herbs to cleanse the birth canal.

Such practices seemed strange to me after being taught Western medical techniques. At first, too, I accepted these practices because I did not want to appear "The Ugly American." In time, I learned to accept and appreciate the indigenous medical practices as an integral component of healing.

In barrios of the Philippines, on Montana Indian reservations, and in urban Philadelphia I have witnessed families sleeping overnight in the hospital on the floor beside the patient. The families help with bathing and care of the patient who feels comforted and calmed by their presence. As Ellen from Labrador told me, "When you are with your own kind, you feel safe."

Claudette Amadon, a chemotherapy nurse at Alaska Native Hospital, was lauded repeatedly by former patients as a person who took time to explain procedures and helped women to overcome their fears. She was seen by others as a caring person and nurse.

Judy Applin-Poole, nurse coordinator with the Newfoundland Cancer Foundation, was also praised by Labradorian women as a "wonderful" person who took sufficient time to allay their fears by being straightforward, by telling things as they were.

In addition, economic status was also an important context. The women in the study were well aware that those who could afford to pay for treatment with private insurance were usually well-treated by the medical community. For those who were poor or on medicare or public assistance, their treatment suffered. They knew that poor minority patients, especially Indian or Native Alaskan, had few chances of being well-treated by the medical community.

Christopher (1993) notes that, while higher levels of income correspond to increased survival rates, "those in low income families who received comprehensive care through a health plan seemed to do as well as wealthier people, suggesting that access to good treatment, rather than some other factor, made the difference (in survival)" (p. 60).

Alaskan women living in Anchorage, however, who were treated by Public Health physicians from Indian Health Service (IHS) complained of the lack of respect demonstrated by physicians within that medical community. In that regard, women treated in the private sector received more respect. Native women from Montana also complained about IHS practices: "They don't understand the culture. The health care providers rotate so that you don't have continuity with physicians. The bureaucracy is slow to change" (interview with an anonymous, native nursing student from Salish Kootenai College, 1994).

Certainly, the role of patriarchal medicine and the images that are evoked in Native Women when dealing with such a system offer much food for thought. Reform here is a must. The present and future health of Native Women depends on it, especially for those susceptible to or already with breast cancer.

Knowing from Our Grandmother's Lives

The Northern Native Women I interviewed want others to know that there is life after breast cancer: life that is rewarding; that makes each survivor more appreciative of each new day, of each birthday and holiday; that maintains connections with the earth, the land, the sunsets, and the animals. The women have adapted to the changes which breast cancer initiates. They have requested to speak these final words to the readers of this book:

Mimi: "Fight for your life. It's so hard."

Ellen: "Have someone speak my language and have a support group."

Lilly: "Get checked out right away. Take care of yourself right from young."

Sally: "Get your lumps checked out right away."

Ingred: "Don't get depressed. Get into a [support] group."

Baby: "Talk out your fears. Don't run [to alcohol and drugs]. Get examined right away. Know your rights."

Fiona: "Be strong. I was in denial for six months."

Glenda: "There is research going on. Don't let anyone talk you into anything."

Linda: "Educate yourself and cover all of your options."

Maxine: "Don't resign your fate. Have a positive attitude."

Joan: "Take time to do what you want to do. Love your family and your friends. It can be taken away so quickly."

These women are both vulnerable and resilient. Their resilience is manifested in their empowerment. They are empowered by their families, by the significance of their contributions to the study, and by the quality of their work and its influence on the lives of others.

In the tradition of "The People," our stories of bravery and risk taking will be told alongside stories of great seal hunters and warriors. The drummers will beat their skin drums and everyone will dance in the "Singing House." Our stories will influence the lives and health of our daughters and our granddaughters.

I also feel the women in this study have adapted to their breast cancer journey. Not only have they adapted culturally by returning to traditional pursuits as a means of healing and therapy, but some have adapted medically by demonstrating risk-taking behavior with adjuvant therapies. They have adapted socially by returning to their families, jobs, or to school. The women have helped others clearly understand their images and feelings of powerlessness associated with the loss of a breast and with a patriarchal medical system. Although they may feel disempowered by the politics and economic inequities of their treatment options, in telling their stories they also feel empowered in helping to define the importance of breasts for women from Northern cultures; cultures, we should recall, much influenced by collision with a more dominant North America. These women have provided a picture of their experiences with breast cancer from their own point of view. There is much more to learn from and with Native women about issues affecting their health. I hope that my work will inspire others to carry out similar research projects.

In the Native North American tradition, elders are the "Keepers of the Wisdom," especially female elders (Hungry Wolf, 1980). In many Native North American cultures, all elder women in the tribe are considered to be grandmothers. Also, all women in the tribe who lived long ago are spoken of as "Grandmother" (Hungry Wolf, 1980). What has been told us by "our grandmothers" have become sacred words. As a result of their horrific experiences historically, they know the words and wisdom that can heal others. "The People showed their respect for the elders . . . they had learned a lesson taught by . . . women they came to love and care for until each died . . ." (Wallis, 1994, pp. 135–136). We should hear the meaning of those words, and take healing and comfort in what they have told us.

THE MAMMOGRAM CONNECTION

When I moved to Montana last year, I brought ten years of my mammogram films. Not only did the brown Manila envelope hold a record of healthy breasts, it also held an unwritten record of lived anxiety, frazzled nerves, and prayers that the X-rays would be normal. I think about women living in the North, especially on the reserves in northern Ontario, and in small villages of Labrador, The Northwest Territories, and Alaska. I think about how they are denied access to mammography by distance and lack of government funding.

"Mammography is the most important tool we have today [in the fight against breast cancer]" (Baker, 1991, p. 35). Nonetheless:

> Screening for breast cancer presents an important clinical policy question for Indian Health Service (IHS). There is evidence that American Indian and Alaskan native women with breast cancer are diagnosed at a more advanced stage of disease and that stage-specific survival is worse than for non-Indian women. (Nutting et al., 1994)

According to epidemiologist Anne Lanier (1993) of Alaska Native Hospital: "Screening for breast cancer, if it is to include mammography, is not something that has been or can be readily available to the Native women in the predominantly rural, remotely scattered communities. . . . It is extremely difficult and costly to offer cancer screening services as currently recommended for the nation"—a disconcerting admission, to say the least! Native women in remote villages deserve the right to be screened just as other women in America do. Recently, Nutting et al. (1994) have studied the five-year effects of mammography screening on Alaskan native women and Indian women. The findings suggest that the total cost of breast cancer is 3.6 times higher with mammography screening, but results in a 27.9% reduction in breast cancer deaths over the first five years of the program.

Portable mammograms are available in the lower forty-eight states. Jet service and plane service is available in most remote areas of the North. Therefore, it would seem cost-effective and possible that portable mammography machines could be taken to remote villages once each year to provide mammography screening, just as it is offered to women in rural areas of the lower forty eight. If the United States government can afford to spend $150,000 on the experimental health care of late stage breast cancer for one woman, how much more cost-effective to preventively screen a number of women in the "at risk" age group. *Healthy People Objectives 2000** targets the reduction of breast cancer to 20.6 cases in 100,000 women as one of its goals. Further, to accomplish that goal, it recommends mammography screening for all women ages fifty to seventy-five.

As American women, this goal applies to Alaskan Native Women as well. It is well-established that cancer screening with mammography can detect tumors two years before they can be palpated by clinical or breast self-exam (Miller, Feuer, & Hankey, 1993). There is no question here that a wiser use of money would be to screen women initially, so that they can undergo more conservative treatments for *in situ* tumors.

> If the increased incidence of breast cancer in women is primarily due to early detection associated with screening by mammography, increased survival and a reduction in mortality are the expected outcome. (Miller, Fueur, & Hankey, 1994)

The American Cancer Society recommends that all women over the age of forty be screened by mammogram every two years and women over fifty be screened by mammogram every year for breast cancer (Weiss, 1992). The cost of a mammogram ranges from about $50 to $200. Thirty-one states now require that private insurance companies pay part of the total cost. In 1990, Medicare began coverage for screening mammography. In 1991, congress moved to remove a payment cap of $55.

> According to the American Cancer Society figures, women who have localized breast tumors have a survival rate of 91% after five years. In comparison, only 69% of women whose cancers have spread beyond the breast survive beyond five years. The survival rate for non-invasive cancer is close to 100%. (DuBoise-LeGrand, 1992)

Although Native American Women have the lowest cancer incidence rate of all races, they present the highest mortality rate (National Alliance of Breast Cancer Organizations).

---

*Healthy People Objectives 2000: National health promotion and disease prevention objectives from the Department of Health and Human Services, Washington, D.C.

In response, in the lower forty-eight funding from AVON cosmetics and The National Alliance of Breast Cancer Organizations is reaching out to educate Native American Women about how mammography and early detection through screening can save their lives.

With a combination of mammography and breast self-exam, increased survival rates could also apply to Northern Native Women. Again and again the strategy which saves lives is early detection.

Currently, in the Northwest Territories, the cumulative travel costs for removing patients to central hospitals in southern Canada is over $21,000,000 (Teleconference, Nov. 24, 1994, Inuit Broadcasting Co.). Some of these costs could be avoided by improving screening in centers that are more geographically accessible to Northern Native Women.

Personal Reflection Continued

As a result of this work, mom and I grew closer, and it happened in a lightning flash on a summer night. Before going to Alaska in the summer of 1994, I visited my stepfather, my dad, after his surgery for prostate cancer. He was in the hospital for over a week. I stayed at my parents' house outside of Boston. They have lived on the second floor of the same canary yellow duplex for over forty years. That night, sleep was elusive for both of us, perhaps due to the heat of that hot June night or to some other ancestral force which kept us awake; we will never know. After coming home from the hospital where the man we both loved slept amid drainage tubes, intravenous bottles, pain medication, and strangers, mom and I sat on the back porch immersed in our own thoughts. The back porch has always been our refuge on hot summer nights. When I was younger, I christened it "Dad's Hooch." On some sweltering nights, I'd drag my sleeping bag out there and sleep on the floor, even as an adult. I'd take comfort in the old maple trees, dark blobs against the sky, and the twinkling of stars light years away. Out there in Dad's Hooch that night, mom and I sat together, light years apart in thought and purpose. Mom knew I'd be leaving soon to interview Native Women in Alaska.

"How was it for you, Mom, I mean when you had your breast cancer? How did Dad react; how did you feel?" I asked. Suddenly Mom became animated and eloquent. She talked freely about her fears of being rejected as a woman and her concerns regarding the medical establishment. For the first time, I saw Mom in a different way. We were talking about things that mattered to both of us. She wanted me to feel her pain and know her experiences. She was a warrior, she was empowered; she helped me to see how she too had suffered as a victim of incompetent medical practices. However, she was quick to indicate that not all doctors are unfeeling.

Magdalen Island, Quebec, Canada–Harp Seal Pup. Photo by the author.

AFTERWORD

*D*uring the summer of 1994, I worked as a field assistant on a tundra botany project in the Chugach Range near Anchorage and at Toolik Lake Research Station one hundred fifty miles from the North Slope of Alaska. Before I began the work as a field assistant in Anchorage, I interviewed the Northern Native Women in Anchorage for this study.

After concluding the interviews, I went hiking alone for days up and down the Chugach mountains to examine the alpine ecosystems and trek across Arctic tundra. The sun burned brightly for over twenty-one hours a day. I thought about my past and my future. At day's end, I'd sit in my tent and write in my journal, including thoughts about the Northern Native women I had interviewed.

Journal Entry   The wind is howling on the saddle ridge and my ankle is killing me from all the hiking. Cloud patterns play tag with the snow capped peaks. Birds twitter. I think about the aromas of the Ledum (Labrador Tea) and Empetrum and remember Ellen uses these plants for her sore throat. I watch where I place my feet in the spongy lichens and wonder where my life has flown. I feel like a kid myself, but my body betrays me with pain. I'm beginning to believe my old Memere when she used to tell me, "Eh, Bientot, ma petite fille, life is short."

Afterword

The Alaska sun is in my face and warm on my back as I dig in the boggy meadows. Snowy peaks all around create the illusion of a bowl. Insects, especially mosquitoes, are my friends. They gather round me like gossiping old women buzzing with secrets. I am their "take out blood lunch" for the day.

Northern Harriers soar above my working space and scream because I am invading their hunting areas. Under the soil where I dig, the land reveals its secrets from the time of glaciers and volcanoes. If I look hard enough, here and there are rings of glacial powder—messages left from the past for us of the future to find and figure out. These earth secrets remind me of ancient ancestors.

Old friends from other tundras are here beside me: crowberry, Labrador Tea, bearberry not quite ripe as they would be later in August. I could be anywhere in the Arctic. The plants are similar in Baffin, Churchill, Scotland, and here on the tundra of Alaska. The hillsides are brilliant with flowering rock gardens and millions of lichens.

Trudging down the valley I feel a kinship with ancient peoples who have gone this way before, Arctic people with ancient secrets and ancestral relationships. Certainly they felt the power and majesty of the land as they gazed on snow covered mountains and picked the same berries that I do. We are all linked together in the great sun circle. I weigh the soils and describe the plants, but it is hard to concentrate and my mind wanders.

The stories I hold from the women swirl around me, cloaked in images of Indian blankets, powerful animal spirits, Micmac grandmothers, the power of the land, and breast cancer.

Clouds over the Brooks Range, a changing landscape of color and light. The midnight sun bright as day makes her circle around the top of the earth just as from the beginning of time. While Philadelphia sleeps, the Arctic throbs with the pulse of life.

A cold Arctic rain pelts down on the tent during the late night—a cold slate grey rain that chills to the bone. Winter is never far from this land. In the morning, loons cry out from the lake and the sun is golden warm in the east.

I hope the weather holds. The helicopter comes tomorrow. I find two wolf scats and put them in plastic bags to bring home, but I haven't seen the wolf. She is too elusive and wary of humans. She leaves bones and scat on the tundra to let me know that this is her place.

Afterword

The last day on the North Slope. Sitting on a high dryas summit surrounded by tundra berries, crowberries, blueberries, and bear berries. They are fat and starting to ripen with the blush of fall. Toolik Lake is an amethyst nestled in the rolling green hills of tundra. The last of the plots have been clipped and soils taken. The mosquitoes are aggressively fierce today, in the hundreds. In the wet meadows of Alaska I am akin to barefoot Asian women in rice paddies. My net hat keeps the mosquitoes from entering my nose and eyes as I work. The Brooks Range wears a misty cloud, but the sun is hot.

On the way down to my tent, a willow ptarmigan in summer plumage crosses my path. It keeps a wary eye on me as I slow to let it scamper through to a clump of willows along the lake.

How like the Arctic animals I have become, willing to accept and adapt to changes, wary yet strong, like the women I have met through the Northern Looking Glass. It has been a long journey, one in which I have resolved my own breast cancer fears. Within the circle of the sun and of life, other women have made me stronger. Other women have cried and have become angry. I will, too. There is healing in the telling of our stories. In the end, we endure, knowing that life is wonderful, mine lived to the fullest adventure. My grandmothers would have been proud.

Appendix A

THE RAINBOW CONNECTION: CONTAMINATION IN NORTHERN ECOSYSTEMS

THE RAINBOW CONNECTION

Personal Reflection

I was twelve. My family had been spending summers at a lake in northern Massachusetts where we owned a cabin. My brother, the neighbor boys, and I were inseparable as we fished, swam, water-skied, picked berries, and played baseball. No matter that I was the only girl. I was included in the boys' culture and games. We used to row a boat to the middle of the lake and dive off . . . until we sank the boat, or almost. I rowed the boat across 1.5 miles with an inner tube inside, while my brother and our friend, Eric, swam across.

That summer, beginning as ant hills and just as much of a nuisance, my nubile breasts became evident little mounds under my T-shirts. I didn't want them. They ached. They set me apart from the boys who were my play-mates. I bound them up with an ace bandage and continued to wear T-shirts. I told what I thought were creative stories when my period restricted me from swimming: "I have poison ivy; I have a sore throat."

In her wisdom, my mother recognized my developing body and bought me a bra. I hid it in my bike bag. I needed and wanted to be included in the culture of the boys. But that summer, they looked at me differently, not as "one of the boys," but as a girl who could pitch like a boy, as a girl who could cast like a boy. They respected me, and continued to include me, because I was their friend, their girl friend.

Today as a grown woman I want my breasts. I like the way they set me apart from the men. I like the way they feel when they are fondled and stroked. I need to care for them. I need to work to improve the polluted environment that may snatch away my pleasure.

I have named this section as "The Rainbow Connection" for a valid reason. Everything in nature is connected to everything else. Every molecule of carbon dioxide and oxygen in the air affects every blade of grass, every animal, and every plant. Whatever contaminants that affect the connection, affects humans. Human health is connected to the environment much like a rainbow that connects sky and earth. Florence Nightingale and Mary Breckinridge* were two nurses whose theories pioneered in this field of thought. In more recent times, Virginia Hamilton and Rachel Carson have reinforced a similar message. More work needs to be done in finding the direct link to breast cancer and the environment. "The parochial roots of science . . . can be seen only through other traditions of women and non-Western peoples. It is these subjugated traditions that are revealing how modern science is . . . and how ecological destruction and nature's exploitation are inherent to its logic. . . . This view of science as a social and political project of modern western man is emerging from the responses of those who were defined into nature and made passive and powerless: Mother Earth, women, and traditional cultures" (Shiva, 1989, p. 21).

Fiona spoke to me of contamination in her food sources in Arctic Alaska, specifically about the nuclear contamination from a waste dump near Point Hope, Alaska: "We hate the White people for what they have done to the caribou and the seals. The caribou come through there and they get sick. Their meat is all black with little holes in it; and the whales

---

*Mary Breckenridge: founder of Frontier Nursing in Kentucky.

come through and they get sick. It makes us all sick if we have to eat these animals. Why don't they come here to clean it up?"

Rubra spoke of contamination of the vegetables that are imported from the southern parts of the United States and Canada: "They are full of pesticides." But, like Fiona and Rubra, many Native women also feel powerless against agrabusiness and their government heirlings. They know very well that: "Of all the stressors affecting a population's health, one of the most devastating is rapid and irrevocable change in a people's way of life" (McElroy & Townsend, 1985).

For Northern Native People, their collision with Western culture began long before the whalers arrived from England and Norway. The health of Northern Native People reflects a long history of contact with explorers, fur traders, whalers, and missionaries. As a result of that contact, the people of the north have suffered from major epidemics of tuberculosis, measles, small pox, whooping cough, and a host of other infections including influenza. "Whatever the business of the contact agents, whether to find a home, to preach the gospel, or to make a profit, they often disrupted the lives of the native people whose worlds they entered. The health of Northern Native People reflects the ways in which they have adapted to the original contact agents as well as to more recent ones" (McElroy & Townsend, 1985).

Only recently have Northern Native People developed an immunity to many of the introduced diseases. As the population of Northern Native People continues to blend their culture with the technology of Western civilization, development and pollution in northern ecosystems will be increased in the form of mining, pesticides, and nuclear waste products. Biological disease and plagues have been followed by chemical contamination and ecologic disaster. "When ecological or cultural change leads to an imbalance in the relationships that make up the ecosystem, the usual adaptive mechanisms [of the population] do not work well" (McElroy & Townsend, 1985, p. 15).

As Western culture continues to blend with that of northern Aboriginal cultures in Canada and Alaska, the people view themselves as victims of contaminating governments and mega-businesses—and all in the name of development. Nor does it end there.

From the Everglades to the Arctic, from Maine to San Diego, Indian Nations are being targeted by waste management companies as potential sites for giant solid waste landfills and hazardous waste incinerators. In response many Indigenous people have pooled their power by uniting socially and politically. Last year, Native Americans gathered north of Rapid City, South Dakota, at a sacred Sioux gathering place, Bear Butte,* to expand their fight against the toxic invasion of their sacred lands (Beasley, 1991). As a result, Native Americans for a Clean Environment (NACE) was instrumental in closing Sequoyah Fuels, a company in eastern Oklahoma which processed uranium for bombs and nuclear reactors. The company had been cited for over 15,000 violations including an accident which released a large cloud of nitrogen dioxide as well as for disposing of tons of nuclear waste which the company renamed "fertilizer" (Ruben, 1993).

The Gwich'in, North America's most northern group of Indian People, also waged a successful battle against drilling the Arctic National Wildlife Refuge (ANWR). The 200,000 member herd of caribou who travel through on their migration to and from the ANWR are the main staple of the economy and chief food source for the Gwich'in (Ruben, 1993).

Organochlorine

Although there is evidence to support environmental contamination as causal in other forms of cancer, establishing an environmental *link* to breast cancer is difficult. Recent data suggest that breast cancer incidence *appears* to be rising among Northern Native Women (Gilchrist, 1993) and the rise parallels contamination of the food chain by radionuclides and organochlorines (Hanson, 1993). There are many other environmental pollutants that have been introduced into the ecosystems of the north from areas of the industrialized nations which could be discussed in this section; however, I believe that two of the most significant and deadly are organochlorines and the radionuclides. Northern Native Women, connected to the land, are well aware of the danger that contamination causes.

---

*On the sacred ground of Bear Butte the Sioux traditionally place prayer flags to link earthbound souls to the Great Spirit.

Organochlorines are chemicals in which at least one atom of chlorine is bonded to carbon containing organic matter. Many chlorines are produced intentionally in industry by reacting chlorine gas with petroleum hydrocarbons. There are an estimated 11,000 organochlorines in commerce, including plastics, pesticides, solvents, refrigerants, and other chemicals (El-Bayoumy, 1992).

Organochlorine or chlorinated hydrocarbon insecticides are part of a broader class of halogenated hydrocarbons, which includes the well-known, troublesome polychlorinated biphenyl (Harte et al., 1991, p. 116).

Women with breast cancer have higher levels of organochlorines in their breast tissue and other tissues than women without breast cancer (Falck et al., 1992). In Canada's St. Lawrence River, where organochlorines are used in the production of paper, the Beluga whale population has demonstrated evidence of increased cancers of the mammary glands. Researchers discovered one lactating female Beluga in the St. Lawrence to have a PCB level of 1.7 parts per million (ppm) in her breast milk, an indication that young belugas ingest large amounts of PCBs right from birth (Fox, 1992). The fish and other marine organisms of the St. Lawrence River swim freely to the ocean and could contaminate other marine organisms through bioaccumulation effects in the food chain. In Labrador and Quebec, native people depend on the marine food chain for subsistence fishing and hunting. If the marine food chain is contaminated, the contamination also affects the human population. For example, it was recently discovered that Native women in Arctic Quebec have a level of 14.7 micrograms of PCBs in their breast milk. These high levels of PCBs make their milk unfit for their children's consumption (1 microgram per ml is "tolerable") (Lowell, 1990). As chlorine contamination of the marine mammals reflects an extension of global pollution, the traditional way of the Inuit, with its ecological wisdom that relies on marine mammals for food, may be altered forever (Lowell, 1990).

According to federal standards in Canada and in the United States, the allowable limit of PCBs considered safe for human consumption is 2 ppm (Thornton, 1993). This is a significant finding since many native people as well as polar bears eat the same fish, seals and walrus, all of which are contaminated with unsafe levels of PCBs. The effects of bioaccumulation (the magnification of toxins in organisms as the toxin moves along the food chain) have become evident in women who live in Northern Quebec (Swain, 1991).

The EPA (Environmental Protection Agency) estimates that ten million pounds of PCBs come into the environment every year because of spills, leaks, and vaporization. As a result, human fat now contains relatively high levels of PCBs. . . . One mother tested in Michigan had over 10 ppm (parts per million) PCBs, a level high enough to cause learning disabilities in monkeys (Samuels & Bennett, 1983, p. 139).

A general principle is that organochlorine compounds tend to accumulate in fat-containing foods, such as meat, fish, dairy products, whereas organophosphates are more common in cereal products . . . (DDT is among the major organochlorines as is Captan, Lindane) . . . another environmental contaminant is the mixture of chlorinated hydrocarbons, called polychlorinated biphenyls, or PCBs. These are found widely in our environment as a result of industrial contamination. The summary of the Diet, Nutrition and Cancer Committee is that PCBs, if taken at high levels, could lead to the development of malignancy in humans. (Rosenbaum, 1983, pp. 134–135)

Among populations of polar bears living above the Arctic Circle, the PCB (polychlorinated biphenyl) contamination is 7 ppm. In polar bears who live below the Arctic Circle, the percent of PCB contamination jumps to 70 ppm (Ramsey, 1993).

When they enter the body, organochlorines can mimic the female hormone estrogen. That can cause deformities (crossed bills in birds of prey) as well as make males act like females (Siddon, 1994).

Brent Palmer, an assistant professor of microanatomy at Ohio University, has been working with double-crested cormorants exposed to PCBs around Green Bay, Wisconsin, near Lake Superior. Many of the birds have crossed bills and other anomalies related to estrogen mimicking.

"There was a 30% drop in breast cancers when carcinogenic pesticides were phased out in Israel, yet none of the cancer establishments '100 million studies' (in the U.S.) has focused on organochlorine pesticides," says Dr. Samuel Epstein, Professor of Occupational and Environmental Medicine, School of Public Health, Illinois Medical Center, Chicago (Usme & Toledo, 1993). Viable proof to link organochlorines with breast cancer

may never be found because of the complex reality of global chemical contamination. Credible science does suggest, however, that organochlorines
may contribute to breast cancer risk. This knowledge has profound implications for millions of women. In public health and environmental policy, the
precautionary principle requires that we provide a preventive framework for
making policy decisions that affect the environment. Prevention should be
the framework for evaluating scientific information and for taking action on
organochlorines (Wolff, Toniolo, Rivera, & Dubin, 1993).

Appendix B

RADIATION

According to the National Research Council (1980) in Washington, D.C., the female breast is one of the organs most susceptible to radiation carcinogenesis.

> Before 1945—before the atomic bomb was dropped on Japan—breast cancer was rare among women in Hiroshima and Nagasaki. When the National Research Council did its study, some thirty years later, breast cancer was not rare at all; it was common, terrifyingly so. (Brady, 1991, p. 8)

Hansen's research (1993) discovered radionuclide behavior in arctic tundra ecosystems to be similar throughout the polar ecosystems. However, there are differences in levels of contamination found in food sources, because of differences in food choice and processing choice by various ethnic groups. Hansen studied radiation ecology in an area of northern Alaska between 66 degrees North Latitude and the Arctic Ocean, constituting about 310,000 square kilometers. Four major caribou herds are found here, the largest aggregation of big game animals in North America. Also in this area are several Inupiat Eskimo and Athabascan Indian villages, representing four major ethnic groups.

Natives of Northern Alaska are members of unique ethnic groups with distinctly different subsistence cultures that substantially affect amounts of fallout radionuclides in their diets. Inland Inupiat (Eskimo) during the 1960s and early 1970s relied on caribou for much (55%–60%) of their food, while coastal Inupiat utilized marine mammals extensively (10%–20% of diet) and caribou and reindeer moderately. (Hansen, 1993, p. 203)

Direct absorption of radionuclides is the most important process in which fallout is concentrated in arctic tundra with lichens being particularly susceptible to contamination (Hansen, 1993). The caribou feed on contaminated lichens which lead to the accumulation of radionuclides in the tissues of the caribou; these ultimately pass on to the humans who eat the contaminated caribou. Fiona was acutely aware of the contamination of the whales and the caribou particularly in the areas near Point Hope, Alaska.

During Autumn, caribou and reindeer gradually shift to their winter diet, composed mainly of lichens, and cesium 137 concentrations in soft tissues begin a steady increase through the winter months (Hansen, 1993). The level of radionuclides was measured in the Inupiat of Anatuvik Pass, Alaska. Levels of Cesium 137 in humans followed the annual migration cycle of the caribou through contaminated areas, demonstrating the fact that the Inupiat are being affected by the radionuclides in caribou meat. (Hansen, 1993)

The radionuclides in the northern ecosystems come from a number of sources: atmospheric testing of nuclear weapons, uranium mining, and both normal and accidental emissions from nuclear power plants, (Hansen, 1993). Support for Hansen's work can be found in the age-adjusted-incidence in breast cancer among Athabascan women living in Central Alaska, who depend on nuclear contaminated caribou meat as their primary protein source (Burhansstipanov, 1993). X-rays used in mammography also may be causal in many breast cancers (Fackelmann, 1993).

Maybe the earth is telling us something. . . . It's a destruction. The stuff is leaking into the St. Lawrence River from the Alcoa plant, the river is trying to fix itself. The fishes who go to the bottom to clean it, they're coming up with their bodies upside down, the belly up. With that kind of sign, they still miss the point of how bad the pollution is. . . . I'm afraid to eat the fish; I won't eat the fish from that river. (Lorraine Canoe, Mohawk: 1993)

Appendix C

RESEARCH DESIGN
AND METHODOLOGY

RESEARCH DESIGN AND METHODOLOGY

Methodology

In designing my study, I use the model of medical ecology within the paradigm of phenomenology and feminist methodologies. The field of medical ecology dovetails with the helping profession of nursing as well as that of medicine. Traditionally female in nature, the helping professions and the environment, with its female Mother Earth image, share a long history of honor, respect, domination, and oppression. Certainly, understanding the environment as a domain of nursing knowledge has been a component of nursing theory since Nightingale (1860) and Breckenridge (1952). In 1978, Fawcett, and more recently in 1987, Kim, identified person, *environment*, health, and nursing as essentially interrelated concepts (in Smith & Maurer, 1995). Leninger (1988) also writes that *culture* must be included as an essential component of nursing and medical education. As a result, medical ecologists examine culture, environment, and clinical and epidemiological data in investigating health and disease. The concept of environmental adaptation through evolutionary mechanisms is a key to medical ecology (Townsend & McElroy, 1995) and grounded in evolutionary theory.

In the present study, I investigate women's lives as a result of their breast cancer journey; how they have evolved, adapted, and become empowered. I examine the image that Northern Native Women have of themselves and their relationships after surviving breast cancer. I probe feelings about contamination of the northern environment and how women perceive the impact of pollution on their environment and food sources. In regard to feminism and its various contexts, I must add that I never thought of myself as a "feminist" until I began to speak with other women about my work. In the years that followed, my work in the environmental field, initial investigations for this study, classes in women's studies, and becoming more familiar with the goals of the women's movement have all contributed to my development, and what I recognize now, as a feminist researcher.

Feminist research contributes to a greater understanding of women's lives. Since women were both the informants and experts here, this investigation is *about* women, not *on* women, and takes into account women's achievements, interests, and experiences (Klein, 1983). Traditional psychosocial research, which arose generally within and from the point of view of White middle class males, also measures experiences from the normative vantage of the male. In this paradigm, with "males as the norm," women have been taken either as sufficiently abnormal to skew the data or have been marginalized as sufficiently similar to men so as not to be considered as appropriate subjects for distinctive research. Nonetheless, and for some time now in response, women have been "creating an alternative definition of themselves, human nature, and experience" (French, 1992, p. 17). Certainly in this project, I have carefully avoided measuring the women involved against the male norm, at least as defined above. On the other hand, I do examine pertinent issues of patriarchy within the male medical model.

Beginning with and involving my own life's experiences within the research is also of some importance here (Reinharz, 1992). I became involved not only as a researcher, but as a woman participating in the research process itself with other women. It is this process, too, which allowed me to define my research questions, gain the trust of the women I interviewed, and lead me to useful data. There is also a commitment to honesty with all of the women who participated in the study. To correct what I take as a false image of a passionless researcher, I include excerpts from my written field journals within the body of the work, and which involve my personal thoughts and feelings. The women I interviewed knew of my emotions as they told their stories. We cried together, became angry together, and laughed together. By sharing these emotions I created a bond with the women and provided an ethic of care in the relationship.

In addition, my investigations involve oral history techniques, a valuable component of phenomenology and feminist methodology. Here, oral history is employed with research subjects considered as "elders," living repositors of memory. Oral history is also a useful technique when research subjects evoke contexts of powerlessness. Certainly, in Western society Northern Native Women have been reduced to what is now a tradition of powerless. As Gluck & Patei (1991, p. 9) reveal:

Oral history begins with talk. Because feminists, like social historians, were initially attracted to oral history as a way of recovering the voices of suppressed groups, they tended to ignore the problematic dimension of language as the basis of oral history.

Communication is a means for gaining power. In Western or androcentric culture, our communication is usually gender-based. As a result, "oral history provides a valuable means of generating new insights about women's experiences of themselves and their worlds" (Gluck & Patei, 1991, p. 11). Women, whose voices are silenced by the power of androcentric communication and oppression, need avenues through which to tell *their* stories, and reach out and be listened to. Who among us can imagine an indigenous woman from Labrador, unable to read or write, delivering a public discourse concerning her medical care in the treatment of breast cancer? Oral history makes this possible, with a woman's experiences contributing as much to knowledge as to possibilities in the development of theory (Meleis, Arruda, Lane, & Bernal, 1994).

In this study as well, listening is dual, a means for recording and interpretation. I begin to hear what women say; I listen to the words of their language as well as to what they have not said. "To hear accurately what women say, [then], we must learn to listen to the unspoken as well as to the dominant words" (Gluck & Patei, 1991, p. 11).

According to Duelli-Klein (1983, p. 110), such listening is a way to be open to the complexities in the moment and "to see things in context." Doing so also requires that one "move out of the realms of discourse and logic that rely on linear and hierarchical conceptions of reality, on dualistic models of human nature and intercourse, on dichotomous modes of thought, discourse, and analysis."

At the same time attention must be focused on the teller:

> [W]e must inquire whose story the interview is asked to tell, who interprets the story. . . . Is the narrator asked what meanings she makes of her experiences? . . . In order to listen, we must attend to the narrator rather than to our own agenda. (Gluck & Patei, 1991, pp. 11–12)

On another level, qualitative feminist research is not done in the abstract or as a mode of pure research, but to bring about social change, to raise consciousness, or to develop policy recommendations (Reinharz, 1992). In this sense, the goals of feminist research also dovetail with the philosophical worldview of native peoples who have traditionally held to the ideal of helping one another. In the past as in modern times, this worldview kept clans alive in times of trial and hunger. Because of this philosophical worldview, the women in the study were eager to help women and to let others know of their experiences. Thus, I have attempted to raise consciousness concerning breast cancer in Northern Native Women and to influence changes in policy of health care providers in granting access to mammography to women of the North.

Yet oral history, as I have suggested, also involves the listener, the researcher, in ways seemingly additional to but personally invested in the process as a whole. Here, too, oral history is circular in that the researcher discovers herself, or something of herself, in the women she interviews (Reinharz, 1992). Duelli-Klein (1983, p. 111) understands this aspect of feminist research quite well, prompting us to "see things as they are: whole, entire, complex . . . in context . . . [and] that we understand and explain our eventful, complex reality within and as part of this matrix."

Oral history, experiential analysis, participant observation, and case study are examples of qualitative methods of research that convey a deeper feeling for more emotional closeness to the person studied (Jayaratne, 1980). However, as in all sciences, there are those who favor one method over another and discount methods that seem to disagree with their philosophy of research methodology. Nevertheless, oral history is especially significant to me because of the numerous breast cancers in my family. It is essential for me to hear the stories of other women, so that I can assimilate the coping mechanisms and survival adaptations of the interpreters.

Discovering the Knowers: Recruiting the Women

What an interesting situation! I found myself trying to contact Northern Native Women to initiate interviews, but pondering how to begin. Although I had many friends in the north, none were in the medical profession. I asked friends for Iqaluit and Pangnirtang whether they knew women with breast cancer. None did. I knew I had to research north of 56 degrees north latitude, so I wrote a letter of inquiry to the Baffin Provincial Hospital in Iqaluit and one of the physicians answered that he had recently operated on a woman and she would love to give me an interview. I was passing through Iqaluit in the summer of 1993 and was excited to meet this first participant. However, because my plane was late, she was left sitting in the hospital lobby for an hour. I don't blame her for leaving. When I attempted to set up another interview, she left me sitting in the hospital lobby while she picked berries or went clamming. I was learning the ways of the North. It was summer, after all, and people needed to be out on the land gathering food for winter.

A television commercial for a telephone company, of all things, helped me to focus my ideas. With the help of telephone information—(area code) 555-1212—operators around the North gave me the names and addresses of hospitals in areas with a population over 4,000.

I began the search in Yellowknife, Northwest Territories, and was directed to Ian Gilchrist, Chief Medial Officer of the Territories. Dr. Gilchrist, who had written to me with interesting statistics of cancer incidence in the Territories and in Greenland, noted that there were few documented breast cancer patients in the Northwest Territories and the distance between them was enormous. Coupled with a lengthy Provincial process in securing a research license, I began to look elsewhere. Judy Applin-Poole, nurse coordinator with the Newfoundland Cancer Foundation Grenfell Regional Health Services in St. Anthony, Newfoundland, indicated that she would help me. Judy used her database to contact Northern Native Women in Labrador who had breast cancer. Judy also made reservations for me at various bed and breakfasts along the north coast of Labrador, as well as helping me with the airline connections.

Appendix C

After Judy secured the permission of five women in Labrador and helped me obtain a research permit from Inuit Health Commission and the Grenfell Regional Health Services, I called each of the five women to set up the interview.

In Anchorage, the process was similar with Claudette Amadon as the liaison. In Anchorage, I did not need a research permit or license.

I made the decision to begin the interviews in Labrador because of its proximity to Philadelphia and because of time constraints. It was essential that I begin my project during the winter holiday break from school. Northern Labrador is accessible by plane, even with the sometimes brutal winter weather conditions, with temperatures falling to minus 53° F. But it is easier to travel during the winter in Labrador than it is in the higher latitudes. Most of the Labradorian women are also fluent in English as well as their native language of Inuktitut, allowing me insight into the interview process without the mediation of an interpreter—a translator can change the meaning of an informant's response.

With financial assistance from the Canadian Embassy in Washington, D.C., oral permission from Inuit Health Commission, and written permission from Grenfell Regional Health Services, Judy Applin-Poole, a public health nurse with the Curtis Memorial Hospital in St. Anthony's, Newfoundland, identified a population of breast cancer positive women in Labrador. The initial contact was made by Judy Applin-Poole. I appealed to the Inuit woman's sense of helping other women by inviting the women to tell me their personal breast cancer experiences. We hope these shared experiences will help other Native women by sharing commonality; that their voices be heard so their suffering and trauma will not be lost. Again, by raising awareness of the personal, biological, and *cultural* needs of Northern Native Women, the northern experience of breast cancer *treatment* may improve and increased sensitivity to environmental pollution may also lead to environmental action, future prevention of pollution, and decreased incidence of breast cancer. To pursue interviews with the women of the North Coast, permission was requested and granted from the Inuit Health Commission (IHC). The Inuit Health Commission gave written permission to the International Grenfell Association. For women served by the Grenfell Regional Health Services, permission was requested and granted from Grenfell Regional Health Services. By granting their permission, the Inuit Health Commission also assured their permission. The women in the study were identified as Inuit by Judy Applin-Poole. For the sake of data consistency, and in order to hear the voices of the Northern Native Women across the north from Labrador to Alaska, I chose face-to-face interviews, rather than interview by telephone.

Interviewing face-to face also aids me in reading body language, in hearing what is not said as well as what is said. It is important for me to meet the women who survived. I want to see their faces, to really know them and to touch them. Face-to-face interviews in Alaska were conducted with women who are Inupiat, Athabascan, or Haida. I did not need permission from any governing body to interview women in Alaska. The face-to-face interviews include eleven women, some of mixed blood, as well as full blood in any of the three language groups. Data from the Alaska Native Hospital has verified their native status. The hospital treats Alaska natives who can claim $\frac{1}{32}$ blood quantum of native ancestry (Amadon interview, 1994). The women from Alaska are at least half native, many are full blood.

Because of Claudette Amadon's work* with the tumor registry at the Alaska Native Hospital and through her work as an oncology nurse in the outpatient department of the hospital, Dr. Ronald Bowerman of the North Slope Borough suggested that she make the initial contact with women to secure their permission for the interview. Amadon contacted her former patients and most gave permission to videotape the interviews. During initial contact with the women, two Haida women from a coastal village asked to be included in the interviews. Interviews among the Haida are significant scientifically—in one village of three hundred persons, thirty elders have suffered from breast cancer. The names of the informers have been changed to protect their true identity. In August of 1994, I visited these courageous women in Anchorage, Alaska.

Thirteen women participated in our study of Northern Native Women and breast cancer. Some live in small villages of Labrador (5:13) and some (8:13) in Anchorage, Alaska, a city of one-quarter million.

I recognize the limitations of my research; the population of women interviewed for the project is small. Although I wanted to include additional women from small villages in Alaska and the Northwest Territories

---

*Claudette Amadon established the first tumor registry for Alaskan Natives. She was able to access names of women who might be interested in participating in the project. It was Dr. Bowerman, however, who initially passed my request on to Claudette Amadon.

of Canada, I was financially unable to support a greater number of interviews. In the Northwest Territories, there are six women who have been diagnosed with breast cancer (Gilchrist, 1993). Considering time and distance to interview these women face-to-face, I have not included women from the Northwest Territories in this study. Nor have I included women from the North Slope Borough of Alaska even though there are two women there who agreed to participate again, I was limited by funding from traveling to the North Slope.

In my inquiry, the women who agreed to participate in the interviews are called informants/knowers. They are the information givers and the knowers of their own breast cancer experiences. Before the first interview, I telephoned each participant. They had been contacted by Judy Applin-Poole or by Claudette, so they knew who I was when I called them. I asked them if they were willing to help me and other native women by telling me their breast cancer experience. By asking for their help, I appealed to their Native women's sense of helping and taking care of others. A few of the women were so excited and eager, they began to tell me their story right on the phone! I thanked them for helping me and other women. I told them that it would be an honor to meet them.

I followed the initial phone call with a confirmation letter which set the date, time, and place for the first meeting. During the telephone meeting, an orientation to the study was discussed with the informer/knower. The informer/knower signed the consent form and completed the application form during the initial stages of the interview.

Because a documentary on breast cancer in the north may be forthcoming as a result of this work, I requested that the interviews be videotaped. For all persons present, videotaping the interviews lends an added dimension of stress to the interview itself. Nevertheless, many of the women were eager to have their interview taped for the sake of educating and helping other women—an additionally empowering aspect of the process for them. It was also heartening to have the videotaped interviews of two women who are in late stage cancer. Consent to videotape was given by all but three women. The women who agreed to the videotape were old (sixty-three) and young (forty) alike. I expected that older women would be uncomfortable with the camera, but they were not. The three women who did not agree to be videotaped—one Inuit, one Athabascan, and one Inupiat—shared several commonalities: each was over fifty-five years old and each felt the need to control the interview situation. All interviews were conducted in English.

INCIDENCE OF BREAST CANCER AMONG
NORTHERN NATIVE WOMEN

Currently, because of a variable and inconsistent definition of *race,* an accurate picture of breast cancer incidence among Native people is unknown. The question of race is a major limitation of the United States census and other questionnaires making it difficult to identify who is indigenous and who is not. In determining the census among Native Americans, the final number of American Indians and Alaskan Natives changes depending on how the question of race is phrased. American Indians and Alaskan natives tend to identify race according to ancestry rather than the required blood quantum or tribal enrollment number (Berhansstipanov, 1993). Because of the problems with the census and reporting of cancer incidence to tumor registries, there is *no single* national database that accurately presents cancer-related incidence data for indigenous peoples. Therefore, the problem of cancer incidence cannot be addressed "officially" by the federal government. For my work it was necessary to rely on the following multiple databases to assess the cancer problem among Canadian Inuit and Alaskan natives.

Dr. Ian Gilchrist, Medical Health Officer in the Northwest Territories, wrote in a letter to my inquiries concerning cancer incidence in the Northwest Territories, "The Northwest Territories has a population of about 58,000; 21,000 of whom are Inuit, and about 11,000 of these persons are Inuit females (approximately half of whom live in the Baffin Region). Given the nature of the age pyramid, only about 5 percent fall into the higher risk ages for breast cancer. Dene population is 9,647; Metis population is 4,090 (Indians whose origins come from French fur trappers and Canadian Indian mothers). There are 22,347 non-native people living in the NWT."

Dr. Gilchrist notes that malignant neoplastic disease had been reportable under Northwest Territory (NWT) legislation since 1989. It was not before that, and many cases which were treated in southern Canada may not have been reported to the NWT Department of Health. Eighteen women in the NWT were identified as breast cancer positive in 1989–1991; nine were non-native, three were Dene (The Athabascan Language Indian Group) and six were Inuit.

DIAGNOSIS AND TREATMENT OPTIONS

In a telephone interview with Dr. Ronald Bowerman, Medical Public Health Officer in the North Slope Borough of Barrow, Alaska, *all* cancers of the breast are diagnosed through palpation (feeling the tumor), since breast screening by mammography is unavailable in most of the northern villages. Because the tumor is palpable, it is an indication that the tumor has been growing for some time. When cancer remains undiagnosed, or diagnosed in its later stages, survival rates are low (Lanier, 1993). In outlying villages, there are few formal support groups for women who have breast cancer. Most women are supported by the women in their family—daughters, sisters or aunts. In Anchorage, treatment options include mastectomy, chemotherapy, lumpectomy, and reconstruction. In remote villages of northern Canada and Alaska, mammography screening is non-existent. In 1993, addressing mammography for women in the North, Anne Lanier, Chief Epidemiologist for the Indian Health Service in Alaska, stated, "Although excellent primary care for acute disorders are provided in the communities by a unique health aide system, it is not cost-effective to offer expensive, highly technical and sophisticated medical procedures in the majority of communities" (Lanier, 1993). This statement is a shocking perception of the position of the U.S. government in addressing *Healthy Indian People Objectives 2000.** When any women in the north develops cancer of the breast, it appears that there are very few treatment options available except radical mastectomy, lumpectomy, or partial mastectomy. Under the Indian Health Service (IHS), the woman has to fly to sites such as Anchorage or other urban areas for surgery. Alternative treatments are unavailable. With palpation the usual method by which the physician or patient discovers her breast cancer, cancer mortality rates are higher in the Alaska

---

*Healthy Indian People Objectives 2000: National Health Promotion and Disease Prevention Objectives, U.S. Department of Health and Human Services, Public Health Service.

Native Health Service than in any other population served by the Indian Health Service (Lanier, 1993). Survival rates are also low because of late stage diagnosis. Palpation, we must remember, is an uncertain method which detects only large, advanced tumors (Lanier, 1993). According to Nurse Eileen _____ in Broughton Island, Northwest Territories, in the outlying settlements of the Canadian north, small health clinics usually have a Women's Wellness Day, but the physician must be shared with other settlements, and the patient may not be seen for six weeks after palpation of the lump. Time is crucial for survival. Timely removal of cancers prevents their spread to other areas of the body.

Inuvik is a Canadian city of 2,800 people located on the Mackenzie River Delta near the Beaufort Sea in the Northwest Territories. In 1992, during a face-to-face interview, a group of nurses who work in the city hospital of Inuvik told me that mammography is not available except in Yellowknife, nearly 700 miles away by plane and over twice that distance by road. The only means of treatment for breast cancer is surgery.

INTERVIEW SCHEDULE

The interview was carried out informally usually at the informant's kitchen table or on the living room floor. The informant would usually take the theme of the question in her own direction by discussing additional issues of importance to her. For example, if I asked about who in their family had cancer, in addition to answering that question the women would tack on several stories about that person or persons. If I asked about making love for the first time after a mastectomy, the woman might introduce or even avoid the subject by telling me about someone she knew who had cancer and whose husband left her.

Although a formal interview schedule was not used, the questions are representative of the interview theme. In asking questions which centered around the woman's early life, I sought to discover her perceived issues of traditional women's work in Indian/Inupiat/Inuit culture. Answers to questions focusing on early life also helped me to gain information concerning how empowered the woman felt, and who were the early influences in her life. Culture-specific associations were important during the interview and in analysis afterward as well. For example, if the woman's answers revolved around hunting, working with the dogs or the dog sled, men may have been more of an influence on her early development. On the other hand, if she told me that she used the ulu and tanned hides or scraped fish, she may have been more influenced by women and women's work. In terms of being more empowered and assertive in behaviors with health-care workers, gender influence was also revealing. Those who were most verbal in their reaction to "bad medicine" were the Haida and Athabascan women who were also most influenced by their mothers or grandmothers. The variable here was education, an empowering force. Haida clans, we should recall, are matrifocal and matrilocal, so women as mothers have a great influence on the education of their children. Baby was Athabascan but was brought up by an American teacher, so she, too, experienced the value of education. Asking questions about early childhood also seemed to relax the informant as she brought back memories of a life then cancer free. Finally, for a true oral history I feel that we must begin with the beginning.

Through the use of disclosure of my own fears of breast cancer, and having been related to Northern Native Women who have experienced breast cancer, I asked the following questions, and allowing for the informants to embellish as they wished.

Can you tell me what life was like here in your community as you were growing up?

When you look back on your youth, what is your earliest memory of you as a child?

I have read about the women who worked in the fish industry or worked with native crafts. Did you work skinning fish and drying fish? Can you tell me about that life?

Did you learn to do traditional tasks? Sew caribou skins? What about hide tanning? Did anyone teach you how to do that?

Can you tell me about going to school in your village?

Can you tell me about what kinds of foods you had while you were growing up?

How old were you when you had your first menses? Was there any special ceremony to celebrate?

Did you mother or some other women teach you about having babies and periods and women's stuff? Can you tell me about that?

How old were you when you had your first child?

Were you married then?

Did you breast feed your children?

When your menses stopped (moon time), how old were you?

How many children do you have? Is that how many times you were pregnant or did some of them die while they were still inside your body?

Have any of them had cancers?

Are your parents alive?

Can you tell me about how they died or what kinds of illness did your mother or father have?

Can you tell me about the health of your brothers and sisters and your mother, father etc?

Did any other women in your family (sisters, aunts, cousins etc?) have breast cancer? Who were they? How did they discover that? Are they living now?

Who found your lump?

Can you tell me about that?

How was the diagnosis made?

Did you have to go out of your village for treatment?

What treatment options were available?

Did you have X-ray (Cobalt) or chemotherapy?

Can you tell me about how that was?

Was there anyone who made you feel better, emotionally, physically?

What were the attitudes and feelings of the family members?

Some women feel sad or very fearful or they wanted to kill themselves. Did you have any of those feelings? How did you feel?

What was your attitude?

Women in my own family were very sad and afraid.

What was the role, if any, of religion, spirituality, rituals and herbal medicine and natural healing, customs and lifestyle? Special foods? Dress? Lighting candles, or herbs, prayers?

How would you have changed things if you had some control over the situation?

Would you have liked to have a woman healer who spoke your own language?

What was it like leaving your community and going to the hospital? Did someone go with you?

Tell me about your rehabilitation. Does someone in the medical field still come to check your health?

What is your greatest fear about your cancer?

I want to ask you some personal questions that would help me to know the attitudes of women and men who have been affected by breast cancer.

After your breast surgery, can you tell me what was it like making love for the first time?

How did your husband respond?

How did you feel about your body?

What would you like to tell other Native women who have breast cancer?

What would you like to see for your own daughters and their possible breast cancer?

Can you tell me about the nurses' role in your cancer treatment, etc?

What would you like to tell the doctors and other medical people who are in charge of breast cancer treatment?

Are there any changes that could improve diagnosis and treatment?

How can we help other women who have breast cancer?

What have you heard about the pollution and the poisoning of the fish in Canada and in Alaska? What would you like to tell others about that?

Is there anything else we should talk about?

Appendix C

These questions are not inclusive, but provided a framework for the interviews.

ETHICS

In consideration of ethical issues of working with human subjects, I presented a form to the women in this study addressing informed consent, confidentiality, and any other ethical subject matters that would be addressed in this study. Applying information from Drew and Hardman (1985), the consent form was developed with the following ethical considerations: voluntarism, legal responsibility, invasion of privacy, and deception. The participants voluntarily agreed to participate in the project. They had free power of choice without fraud, duress, or coercion. The participants were legally responsible for themselves and were of sound mind. The project, as they understood it, would not cause them physical harm or allow for invasion into their privacy. The actual names of the women, their villages, or people close to them would not be used. There would be no attempt at deception concerning the study, what the data would be used for and what outcomes were expected. The consent form was reviewed by a number of researchers working with human subjects and they found to be sound.

All but one of the informants was able to sign the consent form. The woman who did not sign gave me verbal consent. Her interview was not audio- or videotaped. All but three of the women were eager for the interview to be videotaped.

On the following pages, a participant information form and a sample consent form are included.

Appendix C

PARTICIPANT INFORMATION FORM

The name you would like me to call you _____

Date _____

Address _____

Telephone (home) _____ (work) _____

Date of birth _____ number of pregnancies _____

When did you first find out that you had a problem with your breast?

_____

When did you first go to the doctor? _____

_____

_____

_____

What kind of treatment did you have? _____

Where you can be reached in the event you change your address?

_____

_____

When did you have your breast treated? _____

Who knows where you will be staying if you move from here? _____

Appendix C

WRITTEN CONSENT FORM

Northern Native Women Speak about Breast Cancer

To the Interpreters in this study:

I am talking to women in Inuvik; Iqaluit; Pangnirtung; Anchorage, Alaska; and Goose Bay, Labrador, who have had a personal experience in surviving breast cancer. You are one of approximately 15 informers.

As part of the study, you are being asked to talk to me for about three hours. During the first hour, we will talk about your life before you knew you had breast cancer; the second hour we will talk about your life once you knew you had cancer; during the third hour we will talk about how you got better.

I want to understand your experience and that of other Northern Native Women who have had breast cancer. I am interested in your life and what your day-to-day experience is like now after having had the experience of breast cancer.

I want women to know that they are not alone.

I want to bring together your ideas so that other women can share in what it is like to be an Inuit woman with breast cancer so that they can be stronger.

Our work will not be related to your medical care.

As part of our work, I may compose the materials from the interviews into a "profile" in your own words. I may wish to use the interview materials for journal articles or presentations to interested groups. I may wish to write a book based on the dissertation. I may want to develop a documentary video.

Each interview will be audiotaped and later written down by me. In all written materials and oral presentations where I may use the interview materials, I will not use your name, names of people close to you or the name of your town. The written part will be typed with initials for names, and in the final form any name you want me to call you will be used.

You may at any time withdraw from the interview process. If you tell me, I will not use any parts about what we have talked about.

If I were to use any of the materials in any way not consistent with what is stated above, I would ask for your permission through additional written consent. In signing this form, you are also assuring me that you will not ask for money for our conversations unless we have agreed on a certain payment.

I, _____ have read the above statement and agree to participate as an interviewee under the conditions stated above.

_____
(Signature of participant)

_____
(Signature of interviewer)

Date: _____

Appendix D

Glossary of Terms

Acadians French Canadian Catholics and decendents who were expelled from Acadie by the British in 1775. Many fled to Louisiana where, today, they are known as Cajuns.

Acadie The name given to the Maritime Provinces by France. Abnaki, Micmac, and Maliseet Indian People lived there.

Adaptation (biological) A genetic mutation in DNA over time which enables the organism to survive changes in the environment.

Alaska Native The term collectively refers to Eskimos, Aleuts, and American Indians who are indigenous to Alaska.

Aleut In Alaska, the people who first inhabited the Aleutian Islands.

American Indian This includes members of federal, state or recognized tribes or people who are self identified as "American Indian" on the U.S. Census. The degree of Indian blood quantum of those who are self-identified is not known. Many tribes have a specific blood quantum requirement for membership, for example ¼; some tribes have a simple dependance requirement.

Antigens Any substance which causes the body to produce anti-bodies with which it reacts.

Bio-accumulation   The magnitude of toxins in organisms as the toxin moves along the food chain.

Blood Quantum   Indicates the percentage of American Indian or Alaska Native. For example, a mother who is 50% or one-half blood quantum is half American Indian and half some other race. If the mother and White father parent a child, the child has a blood quantum of 25% or ¼. Some persons may be of mixed American Indian tribal descendence and must indicate the principle tribe on the Census and other questionnaires.

Cancer Incidence Rate   Refers to a rate, based on identification of new cases of a specific disease (cancer) occurring in a defined population over a certain period.

Cancer Mortality Rate   Refers to a rate based on the number of deaths occurring during a certain time period in a defined population; rates are calculated as number of deaths per 100,000 population per year.

Cancer Survival Rate   Represents the likelihood that a patient will not die from causes associated specifically with their cancer at some specified time after the diagnosis (Miller, B. A., Hankey, B. F., Kosary, C. L., & Edwards, B. K. (Eds.) *Cancer Statistics Review: 1973–1989*. National Cancer Institute. Pub. No. (NIH) 92-2789, 1992, p. 1.

Caribou   (Ranger rangerfer) and Reindeer (Ranger tarandus): a member of the deer species found in the Arctic. Both animals are felt by scientists to be the same species. Reindeer is the Old World term; caribou is the term in North America. Reindeer are found in domesticated groups. In North America, caribou run free and migrate. Reindeer are domesticated caribou.

Cobalt   Radiotherapy using radiation from a cobalt machine.

Culture   A form or stage of civilization as of a certain nation or period.

Etiology   The causes of a disease.

Fallout radionuclides   Radioactive material from atmospheric testing and nuclear accidents.

First Nations   The organized nations in North America of indigenous peoples before contact with Europeans which continues today.

Free radicals   Molecules that lack electrons and seek to acquire them from near-by molecules.

In situ   A tumor which has not spread to other areas. The tumor is not in the milk duct of the breast.

Interleukin   A factor that stimulates the growth of specific types of lymphocytes.

Interferon   Potent natural proteins (alpha, beta, gamma) produced by lymphocytes of the body as the "front line" defense against viral infections; used as a form of immunotherapy against certain cancers and leukemias.

Inuit   Eskimo, Eastern Canadian Arctic. The term means *The First People.*

Inuktitut   The language of the Arctic Inuit, usually written in syllabics.

Inupiat   Eskimo, Alaska, USA.—The people who first settled the Arctic coast of Alaska. They followed the Dorset people.

kamiks   Waterproof knee-high boots made of seal skins with embroidered felt inner liners; traditionally worn only by hunters.

komatik   Dog team sled: for Inuit living below the tree line the sled was made from spruce; for Inuit on the tundra, the sled runners were made of frozen fish, caribou antlers and tied together with sinew; pulled by dog teams and in modern times pulled by snow machines.

komatik box   A wooden box with sides secured to the komatik for carrying game, people, or whatever.

Lymphocytes   White blood cells that are responsible for a variety of immune reactions.

Medical ecology   Defined by McElroy and Townsend (1995) as an approach to research which emphasizes the health implications of interaction between human groups [cultures] and their physical [abiotic], and biological environment. The dynamic concept of the ecosystem helps in understanding how environmental changes and fluctuations affect patterns of disease. Using the medical ecology model, one can study how human technology sets off environmental changes that affect health.

North   Operationally defined for this work, North is considered to begin at 56 degrees north latitude and extend to the North Pole.

Non-Natives   Refers to people who are not recognized as, nor do not identify themselves as North American Indian or Alaskan Native or Inuit/Yup'ik, or Inupiat.

Potlatch   In the Northwest Coastal Tribes of Canada and the United States: In the past, the codes that people lived by were defined by public opinion. There were no written documents and all changes to the existing order were made at potlatches and feasts. All marriages, deaths, adoptions etc. were recorded at the potlatch. Today, although modified, the potlatch is a ceremonial feast which lasts for several days with dancing and feasting. The giver of the potlatch gives away all his goods. It takes many years to prepare for the potlatch, to make or purchase the gifts of silver bracelets, sweaters, blankets or what ever is to be given away; to prepare the food and to prepare the dancers.

Singing House   A special building where, on long Arctic nights, the traditional people would gather around the storytellers for stories of hunting, of bravery.

Society   A closely integrated group of social organisms of the same species held together by mutual dependence and exhibiting a division of labor.

Total breast reconstruction   A surgical procedure after mastectomy in which the surgeon replaces the breasts with a plastic bag containing silicone, or saline, under a skin flap on the chest.

ulu   The Inuit woman's curved knife used for skinning animal hides. Each area of the Arctic has its own special handle design.

BIBLIOGRAPHY

Introduction

Benner, P. (Ed.). (1994). *Interpretive phenomenology.* Thousand Oaks, CA: Sage.

Munhall, P. L., & Boyd, C. O. (1993). *Nursing research: A qualitative perspective.* New York: NLN Press.

Reinharz, S. (1991). *Feminist methods in social research.* New York: Pergmamon Press.

Chapter One

Arsenault, B. (1975). *Histoire et geneaologie des Acadiens.* Ottawa, Ontario, Canada: Lemeac.

Gouguen, A. (1969). *La famille Gouguen.* Moncton, New Brunswick, Canada: L'Evangeline.

Harney, M. P. (1974). *The Catholic Church through the ages.* Boston: St. Paul Books.

Hebert, R. H. (undated). *P'tit Francois Arsenault of Cocagne and his children, 1256,* Unpublished archival material Cocagne, New Brunswick, Canada.

Kennedy, J. H. (1950). *Jesuit and savage in New France.* New Haven, CT: Yale University Press.

Kenton, E. (1927). *The Jesuit relations and other documents. Vol II. The Indians of North America.* Rahway, NJ: Harcourt Brace.

Leger, D. F. (undated). *Histoire de la paroisse Ste. Peirre de Cocagne.* Moncton, New Brunswick, Canada: L'Evangeline.

Macnutt, W. S. (1965). *The Atlantic provinces: The emergence of colonial society 1712–1857.* Toronto, Ontario, Canada: McLelland & Stewart.

Bibliography

Maillard, P. A. S. (1863). Lettre a Madam Drucourt. *Les Soirees Canadiennes*, 299–301.

Paul, D. N. (1993). *We were not the savages: A Micmac perspective on the collision of European and aboriginal cultures*. Halifax, Nova Scotia, Canada: Nimbus.

Stanley, G. (1965). *New France: The last phase 1744–1760*. Toronto, Ontario, Canada: McLelland & Stewart.

Sulte, M. (1881). The mobile camp of 1649. *La Revue Canadienne*. No publisher listed.

Talbot, F. (1935). *Saint among savages*. New York: Harper Brothers.

Thwaites, R. G. (Ed.). (1896–1901). *The Jesuit relations and allied documents (Vols. 1–73)*. Cleveland, OH: Burrows.

Trigger, B. (1981). The Ontario epidemics of 1634–1640. In S. Kreech (Ed.), *Indians, animals and the fur trade*. Athens: University of Georgia Press.

Whitehead, R. H. (1994). *Micmac medicine man*. Halifax, Nova Scotia, Canada: Nimbus.

Chapter Two

Allen, P. G. (1992). *The sacred hoop*. Boston: Beacon Press.

Billson, J. M. (1988, August). Social change, social problems, and the search for identity: Canada's northern native peoples in transition. *The American Review of Canadian Studies*, 294–316.

———. (1995). *Keepers of the culture: The power of tradition in women's lives*. New York: Lexington Books.

Billson, J. M., & Mancini, K. M. (1996). *Inuit women: A century of change*. Used with permission.

Brody, H. (1987). *Living Arctic: Hunters of the Canadian North*. Seattle: University of Washington Press.

Conrad, C., Finkle, A., & Jaenin, C. (1883). *History of the Canadian peoples*. Toronto, Ontario, Canada: Copp Clark Pitman.

Crnkovich, M. (Ed.). (1989). *"Gossip": A spoken history of women in the North*. Ottawa, Ontario: Canadian Arctic Resources Committee.

Chance, N. A. (1990). *The Inupiat and Arctic Alaska: An ethnology of development*. Fort Worth: Holt, Reinhart & Winston.

Crowdog, M. (1990). *Lakota woman*. New York: Harper Perennial.

DeMaille, R. J. (1987). *Sioux Indian religion, tradition and innovation*. Oklahoma City: University of Oklahoma Press.

Dumond, D. E. (1987). *The Eskimos and Aleuts*. London: Thames and Hudson.

Fineup-Riordan, M. (1990). *Eskimo essays: Yup'ik lives and how we see them*. Rutgers, NJ: Rutgers University Press.

Griffen, N. M. (1930). *The roles of men and women in Eskimo culture*. Chicago: University of Chicago Press.

Harrison, S. (1991). *Mother Earth Father Sky*. New York: Avon.

Harrison, S. (1993). *My sister the moon*. New York: Avon.

Bibliography

Hughes, D. J. (1975). *Ecology in ancient civilization*. Albuquerque: University of New Mexico Press.

Jorgenson, J. G. (1973). *The Sun Dance Religion*. Chicago: University of Chicago Press.

Kelly, J. H. (1978). *Yaqui women: Contemporary life histories*. Lincoln: University of Nebraska Press.

Kilunik, M. (1990). Dogs barking. In M. Crnkovich (Ed.), *"Gossip": A spoken history of women in the North*. Ottawa, Ontario: Canadian Arctic Resources Committee.

Langdon, S. J. (1993). *The Native people of Alaska*. Anchorage, AK: Greatland Graphics.

Lantis, M. (1988). *Eskimo childhood and interpersonal relationships*. American Ethnological Society Monograph 33.

Leacock, E. (1991). Montagnais women and colonization. In *Rethinking Canada: The promise of women's history*. Toronto: Copp Clark Pitman.

Linderman, F. (1990). *Pretty shield: Medicine women of the Crows*. Lincoln: University of Nebraska Press.

Masci-Taylor, C. G. N. (Ed.). (1995). *The anthropology of disease*. New York: Oxford University Press.

McElroy, A., & Townsend, P. K. (1995). *Medical anthropology in ecological perspective*. Boulder, CO: Westview Press.

Morrison, B., & Wilson, R. (Ed.). (1992). *Native peoples: The Canadian experience*. Toronto, Ontario, Canada: McLellean & Stewart.

Nelson, R. (1983). *Make prayers to the raven*. Chicago: University of Chicago Press.

Neithammer, C. (1977). *Daughter of the earth: The lives and legends of American Indian women*. New York: MacMillan.

Norman, H. (1990). *Northern tales*. New York: Pantheon Books.

Salisbury, O. M. (1983). *The customs and legends of the Thlinget Indians of Alaska*. New York: Bonanza Books.

Strong-Boag, V., & Fellman, A. C. (1991). *Rethinking Canada: The promise of women's history*. Toronto, Ontario, Canada: Copp Clark Pitman.

Van Kirk, S. (1991). Montagnais women and the Jesuit program for colonization. In V. Strong-Boag & A. C. Fellman (Eds.), *Rethinking Canada: The promise of women's history*. Toronto, Ontario, Canada: Copp.

Roughsey, L. E. (1984). *An aboriginal mother tells of the old and the new*. New York: Penguin Books/Clark Pitman Ltd.

Salisbury, O. M. (1983). *The customs and legends of the Thlinget Indians of Alaska*. New York: Bonanza Books.

Thomas, M. E. (1990). Traditional practice in a contemporary family. In M. Crnkovich (Ed.), *"Gossip": A spoken history of women in the North*. Ottawa, Ontario: Canadian Arctic Resources Committee.

Thomsen, M. L. (1990). Inuit women in Greenland and Canada: Awareness and involvement in political development. In M. Crnkovich (Ed.), *"Gossip": A spoken history of women in the North*. Ottawa, Ontario: Canadian Arctic Resources Committee.

Whitehead, R. H. (1994). *Micmac medicine man*. Halifax, Nova Scotia, Canada: Nimbus.

Bibliography

Chapter Three

Baker, N. (1991). *Relative risk.* New York: Viking Press.

Butler, S., & Rosenblum, B. (1991). *Cancer in two voices.* San Francisco: Spinsters.

Birkeland, J. (1993). Ecofeminism, linking theory and practice. In G. Gaard (Ed.), *Ecofeminism: Women, animals and nature.* Philadelphia, PA: Temple University Press.

Chase, C., & Ford, B. (1978). *Times of my life.* New York: Harper & Row.

Clyne, R. (1989). *Cancer, your life, your choice.* Wellingborough, England: Thornsons.

Finger, A. (1990). *Past due: A story of disability, pregnancy and birth.* Seattle, WA: Seal Press.

Ireland, J. (1987). *Life wish.* Boston: Little, Brown.

Kaye, R. (1991). *Spinning straw into gold: Your emotional recovery from breast cancer.* New York: Fireside Press.

Kahn, F. (1993). *If my breasts could talk* [A dance/mime performance]. Philadelphia: Shubert Theater.

Kushner, R. (1975). *Breast cancer: A personal history and investigative report.* New York: Harcourt Brace Jovanovich.

Lorde, A. (1980). *The cancer journals.* London: Sheba Feminist Publishers.

Metzger, D. (1978). *Tree.* Berkeley: Wingbow Press.

Murcia, A., & Stewart, B. (1989). *Man to man.* New York: St. Martin's Press.

Orenberg, C. (1981). *DES: The complete story.* New York: St. Martin's Press.

Otkay, J., & Walter, C. (1991). *Breast cancer in the life course: Women's experiences.* New York: Springer.

Rollins, B. (1976). *First you cry.* New York: Lippincott.

Shiva, V. (1993). *Staying alive.* Trowbridge, England: Dostesios.

Spence, J. (1986). *Putting myself in the picture: A political, personal and photographic autobiography.* London: Camden Press.

University of Pennsylvania (Producer). (1993). *On the front line against cancer* [Video]. Available from Video Productions, Philadelphia.

Wadler, J. (1992). *My breast: One woman's cancer story.* New York: Addison-Wesley.

Wilkinson, S., & Kitzinger, C. (1991). *Whose breast it is anyway? A feminist consideration of advice and "treatment" for breast cancer.* Paper presented at the Women's Studies Network Conference, London, England.

Williams, T. T. (1992). *Refuge.* New York: Random House.

Williamson, M. (1993). *A woman's worth.* New York: Random House.

Chapter Four

Boas, F. (1901). The Eskimos of Baffin Land and Hudson Bay. *Bulletin of the American Museum of Natural History, 15,* 1–259.

Bibliography

Boase, K. (1989). The Spanish flu. In D. Saunders (Ed.), *Them days: Stories of life in early Labrador, 14*(2). Grand Falls, Newfoundland, Canada: Robinson-Blackmore.

Boik, J. (1995). *Cancer and natural medicine: A textbook of basic science and clinical research.* Portland: Oregon Medical Press.

Butler, S., & Rosenblum, B. (1991). *Cancer in two voices.* San Francisco: Spinsters.

Cameron, E. (1991). Protocol for the use of vitamin C in the treatment of cancer. *Medical Hypothesis, 36*(3), 190–194.

Cameron, E., & Campbell, A. (1991). Innovation vs quality control: An "unpublishable" clinical trial of supplemental Ascorbate in incurable cancer. *Medical Hypothesis, 36*(3), 185–189.

Cameron, E., & Pauling, L. (1976, October). Supplemental ascorbate in the supportive treatment of cancer. I. Prolongation of survival times in terminal human cancer. *Proceedings of the National Academy of Cancer, USA, 10,* 3685–3689.

Cameron, E., & Pauling, L. (1979). *Cancer and vitamin C.* Menlo Park, CA: Linus Pauling Institute of Science.

Chance, N. A. (1990). *The Inupiat and Arctic Alaska: An ethnography of development.* Fort Worth: Holt, Rinehart and Winston.

Creasey, W. A. (1985). *Diet and cancer.* Philadelphia: Lippencott.

Chard, S. (1978). Tribute to Aunt Bertha. In D. Saunders (Ed.), *Them days: Stories of early Labrador, 4*(1), 56–58. Grand Falls, Newfoundland, Canada: Robinson-Blackmore.

Crnkovich, M. (1990). *"Gossip": A spoken history of women in the North.* Ottawa, Ontario: Canadian Arctic Resources Committee.

Dumond, D. E. (1987). *The Eskimos and Aleuts.* London: Thames and Hudson.

Erlich, P. (1957). *Collected Papers* (2 volumes, F. Hemmelwait, Ed.). New York: Pergamon Press.

Getting Along in Labrador. (1975). Calgary, Alberta: Petro-Canada.

Grenfell, W. (1911). *Down north on the Labrador.* New York: Fleming H. Revell.

Grenfell, W. (1932). *Forty years for Labrador.* Boston: Houghton Mifflin.

Grenfell, W. (1934). *The romance of Labrador.* New York: Houghton Mifflin.

Fineup-Riordan, M. (1990). *Eskimo essays: Yup'ik lives and how we seen them.* Rutgers, NJ: Rutgers University Press.

Hennekens, H. (1986). Vitamin A anologs in cancer chemoprevention. In *Important advances in oncology.* Philadelphia: Lippencott.

Hensen, D. V., Block, G., & Levine, M. (1991). Ascorbic acid: Biological functions and relation to cancer. *Journal of the National Cancer Institute, 83*(8), 547–550.

Langdon, S. J. (1993). *The Native people of Alaska.* Anchorage, AK: Greatland Graphics.

Lanier, A. P. (1993, October, November, December). Epidemiology of cancer in Alaska Natives. *Alaska Medicine,* 240–272.

Labrador and Newfoundland Travel Guide. (1993). St. John's Newfoundland, Canada: Department of Tourism and Culture.

Bibliography

Menkes, J. et al. (1986). Serum beta carotine, vitamins A and E, Selenium, and the risk of lung cancer. *New England Journal of Medicine, 315,* 1250–1254.

Minor, K. (1992). *Issumatug, learning from the traditional healing wisdom of the Canadian Inuit.* Halifax, Nova Scotia, Canada: Fernwood.

Rasmussen, K. (1961). *Beyond the high hills.* Cleveland, OH: World.

Saunders, D. (Ed.). (1981). *Them days: Stories of early Labrador.* Grand Falls, Newfoundland, Canada: Robinson-Blackmore.

Simone, C. B. (1992). *Cancer and nutrition.* Garden City Pk., NY: Avery.

Spencer, R. F. (1959). *The North Alaskan Eskimo: A study in ecology and society.* Washington, DC: U.S. Government Printing Office.

Spencer, R. F. (1976). *The North Alaskan Eskimo: A study in ecology and society.* New York: Dover.

Sporn, D. J. (1983, October). Retinoids and suppression of carcinogenesis. Hospital practice. *National Cancer Institute,* 83–98.

Steadman, J. (1993). Nursing at Nain. In D. Saunders (Ed.), *Them days: Stories of early Labrador, 19*(1). Grand Falls, Newfoundland, Canada: Robinson-Blackmore.

Varmus, H., & Weinberg, R. A. (1993). *Genes and the biology of cancer.* New York: W.H. Freeman.

Yonemoto, R. H., Chretien, P. B., & Fehniger, T. F. (1976). Enhanced lymphocyte blastogenesis by oral ascorbic acid. *American Society of Clinical Oncologists, 17,* 288.

Chapter Five

Acker, J., Barry, K., & Esseveld, J. (1983). Objectivity and truth. *Women's Studies International Forum, 6*(4), 423–435.

Adler, T. (1994). Study reaffirms tamoxifen's dark side. *Science News, 145,* 356.

Alagna, S., Morokoff, P., Bevett, J., & Reddy, D. (1987, December). Performance of breast self examination by women at high risk for breast cancer. *Women and Health, 12,* 29–46.

Bailer, J. et al. (1991). *Monitoring human tissues for toxic substances.* Washington Research Council. Washington, DC: National Academy Press.

Baker, N. (1991). *Relative risk.* New York: Penguin books.

Belenkey, M. F., Clinchy, B. Mc V., Goldberger, N. R., & Tarule, J. M. (1986). *Women's ways of knowing: Development of self, voice and mind.* New York: HarperCollins.

Beasley, C. (1991, November, January). Dances with garbage. *E Magazine,* 39–58.

Benner, P., & Wrubel, J. (1989). *The primacy of caring stress and coping.* Menlo Park, CA: Addison-Wesley.

Birkland, J. (1993). Ecofeminism, linking theory and practice. In G. Gaard (Ed.), *Ecofeminism: Women, animals and nature.* Philadelphia, PA: Temple University.

Bostwick, J. (1989, January, February). Breast reconstruction following mastectomy. *CA-Cancer Journal for Clinicians, 31*(1), 40–49.

Bibliography

Bove, F., Fulcomer, M., & Klotz, J. (1993). *Population based surveillance and etiological research of adverse reproductive/tab outcomes and toxic wastes.* Trenton: New Jersey Department of Public Health.

Boyle, J. S., & Andrews, M. M. (1989). *Transcultural concepts in nursing.* Boston: Little, Brown.

Breast fears fade. (1993, November). *Prevention, 45,* 18–20.

Brinker, N. (1991). *The race is won one step at a time: My personal struggle—and every woman's guide—to taking charge of breast cancer.* New York: Simon & Shuster.

Breckenridge, M. (1952). *Wide neighborhoods. A story of the frontier nursing service.* New York: Harper.

Bullough, B. (1981, June). Nurses as teachers and support persons for breast cancer patients. *Cancer Nursing, 4*(3), 224–226.

Burhansstipanov, L. (1993). *Documentation of the cancer research needs of American Indians and Alaska Natives.* Washington, DC: National Institutes of Health, National Cancer Institute, U.S. Department of Health and Human Services.

Bushy, A. (Ed.). (1991). *Rural nursing (Vol. 2).* Newbury Park, CA: Sage.

Butler, S., & Rosenblum, B. (1991). *Cancer in two voices.* San Francisco: Spinsters.

Carpio, B. A., & Majumdar, B. (1993, Winter). Experiential learning: An approach to transcultural education for nursing. *Journal of Transcultural Nursing, 4*(2), 4–11.

Carson, R. (1962). *Silent spring.* Grenwich CN: Fawcett Crest.

Cooper, G. M. (1993). *The cancer book.* Boston: Jones & Bartlett.

Christopher, J. R. (1990). *School of natural healing.* Springfield, UT: Dr. Chris Publications.

Coward, D. (1990). The lived experience of self-transcendence in women with breast cancer. *Nursing Science Quarterly, 3,* 162–169.

Creasy, W. A. (1985). *Diet and cancer.* Philadelphia: Lippencott.

Crnkovich, M. (Ed.). (1990). *"Gossip": A spoken history of women in the North.* Ottawa, Ontario: Canadian Arctic Resources Committee.

Damon, A. (1977). *Human biology and ecology.* New York: W.W. Norton.

Dan, A. J. (1994). *Reframing women's health.* Thousand Oaks, CA: Sage.

D'Angelo, T. M., & Gorrell, C. R. (1989). Breast reconstruction using tissue expanders. *Oncology Nursing Forum, 6,* 23–27.

Danforth, D. et al. (1990). Effect of preoperative chemotherapy on mastectomy for locally advanced breast cancer. *Annals of Surgery, 56,* 6–11.

Davidson, D. B. (1980, April). Is breast cancer the same in men as it is in women? *Cancer Nursing, 3*(2).

Dowling, C. D., & Fineman, D. (1994, May). Fighting back. *Life, 17,* 78–88.

Ekbom, A., Trichopoulous, D. et al. (1992). Evidence of prenatal influences on breast cancer risk. *Lancet, 340,* 1015–1018.

Bibliography

Fabrega, H. (1974). *Disease and social behavior: An interdisciplinary perspective.* Cambridge, MA: MIT Press.

Fett, J. D. (1995, October). Indian self governance: Going through the compacting process. *The IHS Provider, 20,* 10.

Fischer, B. et al. (1983). Influence of tumor estrogen and progesterone levels on the response of tamoxifen and chemotherapy in primary breast cancer. *Journal of Clinical Oncology, 1,* 227–241.

Fowler, M. (1989). Meeting the psychologic need of the breast reconstructive patient. *Plastic Surgical Nursing, 9,* 129–130.

Fox, S. et al. (1987). Breast cancer screening recommendations: Current status of women's knowledge. *Family and Community Health, 10,* 39–50.

Fonow, M., & Cook, J. A. (Eds.) (1991). *Beyond methodology: Feminist scholarship as lived research.* Bloomington: University of Indiana Press.

Freeman, L. J. (1982). *Nuclear witnesses.* New York: W.W. Norton.

French, M. (1992). *The war against women.* New York: Ballantine books.

Galanti, G. A. (1991). *Caring for patients from different cultures.* Philadelphia: University of Pennsylvania.

Gammon, M., & John, E. (1993). Recent etiologic hypotheses concerning breast cancer. *Epidemiologic Reviews, 15*(1), 163–168.

Gapstur, S. M. et al. (1992). Increased risk of breast cancer with alcohol consumption in postmenopausal women. *American Journal of Epidemiology, 136,* 1221–1231.

Giger, J. N., & Davidhizar, R. E. (1991). *Transcultural nursing.* St. Louis: Mosby Year Book.

Griffith, J., Duncan, R. et al. (1989). Cancer mortalities in US counties with hazardous waste sites and groundwater pollution. *Archives of Environmental Health, 44,* 69–74.

Grivetti, L. E. (1992, March, April). The clash of cuisines: The clash of European foods and diet with the Native American cuisines. *Nutrition Today, 27,* 13–15.

Gorman, C. (1993). Breast cancer politics. *Time, 142,* 74.

Harris, J., Lippman, M. et al. (1992). Breast cancer. *The New England Journal of Medicine, 327,* 319–328.

Hellhake, D., & Helgerson, S. D. (1992). Cancer incidence and survival among American Indians registered for Indian Health Service care in Montana. *Journal of the National Cancer Institute, 84*(19).

Hilleman, B. (1993). Concerns broaden over chlorine and chlorinated hydrocarbons. *Chemical and Engineering News, 71*(16), 11–20.

Holden, C. (1994). Western science finds a pearl. *Science, 266*(23), 1949–1959.

Hughes, C. C. (1965). Under four flags: Recent culture change among the Eskimos. *Current Anthropology, 6,* 3–69.

Hungry Wolf, B. (1982). *The ways of our grandmothers.* New York: Quill.

Bibliography

Hurlich, M. (1976). *Environmental adaptation: Biological and behavioral responses to cold in the Canadian sub-Arctic.* Unpublished doctoral dissertation, Anthropology Department, State University of New York, Buffalo.

Kahn, J. (1994, June). Scientists link damaged DNA with breast cancer. *Clinical Chemistry News, 20*(6), 1–10.

Kahn, P. (1990, May, June). Food safety in an era of immune suppression: Is it a problem in the food processing environment? *Nutrition Today, 23,* 16–20.

Kaufmann, K. (1984). Abortion, a woman's matter. In R. Arditti, R. Duelli-Klein, & S. Minden (Eds.), *Test tube women.* London, England: Pandora Press.

Kaye, R. (1991). *Spinning straw into gold.* New York: Lamppost Press.

Kelsey, J. L., & Gammon, M. D. (1991, May, June). The epidemiology of breast cancer. *CA-Cancer Journal for Clinicians, 42*(3), 146–158.

Kelsey, J., & Horn Ross, P. (1993). Breast cancer: Magnitude of the problem and descriptive epidemiology. *Epidemiologic Reviews, 15*(1), 7–16.

Kushner, R. (1982). *Why me?* Philadelphia: Saunders Press.

Lanier, A. P. (1986). Death from cancer in Alaska. *Alaska Medicine, 28,* 57–60.

Lanier, A. P. (1993, October, November, December). Epidemiology of cancer in Alaska natives. *Alaska Medicine, 35,* 240–272.

Lanier, A. P., Bulkow, L., & Ireland, B. (1989). Cancer in Alaskan Indians, Eskimos, and Aleuts: Implications for etiology and control. *Public Health Reports, 104,* 658–664.

Lanier, A. P., & Hart Hanson, J. P. (1985, January). Cancer in the Arctic. *Arctic Policy Review,* 10–11.

Lanier, A. P., & Knutson, L. (1986). Cancer in Alaskan natives: A fifteen year summary. *Alaska Medicine, 28,* 37–41.

Lanier, A. P., & Mostow, E. N. (1991). Screening for cancer in remotely populated regions—lessons from mammography and breast cancer. *Proceedings of the 8th International Congress on Circumpolar Health,* 462–464.

Larson, P. (1984). Important nurse caring behaviors perceived by patients with cancer. *Oncology Nursing Forum, 11*(6), 46–50.

Laszlo, J. (1987). *Understanding cancer.* New York: Harper & Row.

Lee, J. S. (1983). Environmental evaluation of the workplace. *Family and Community Health, 6*(1), 16–23.

Leininger, M. M. (1988). Leininger's theory of nursing: Cultural care diversity and universality. *Nursing Science Quarterly, 1*(4), 175–181.

Leininger, M. M. (1991). *Culture care diversity and universality: A theory of nursing.* New York: National League for Nursing.

LeGrand, E., & Duboise, G. (1992, October). Breast cancer update. *The Nursing Spectrum: Pennsylvania Edition, 1*(2), 4–5.

Lorde, A. (1980). *The cancer journals.* London: Sheba Feminist Publishers.

Love, S. (1990). *Dr. Susan Love's breast book.* Reading, MA: Addison-Wesley.

Bibliography

McDowell, J. (1993, August 30). Straight talk on breast cancer. In *For women first.* Englewood Cliffs, NJ: Bauer.

McElroy, A., & Townsend, P. K. (1995). *Medical anthropology in ecological perspective.* Boulder, CO: Westview Press.

McMurry, B. (Ed.). (1994). *Annual review of women's health.* New York: NLN Press.

Metzger, D. (1978). *Tree.* Berkeley, CA: Wingbow Press.

Milan, A. R. (1980). *Breast self examination.* New York: Liberty.

Miller, B. A., Feuer, E. J., & Hankey, B. F. (1993, January, February). Recent incidence trends for breast cancer in women and the relevance of early detection: An update. *CA-A Cancer Journal for Physicians, 43*(1), 27–40.

Minor, K. (1992). *Issamatuq: Learning from the traditional healing wisdom of the Canadian Inuit.* Halifax, Nova Scotia, Canada: Fernwood.

Moore, L. G., Van Arsdale, P. W., Glittenberg, J. E., & Aldrich, R. A. (1993). *The bicultural basis of health.* Prospect Hills, IL: Waveland Press.

Mostow, E. N., & Lanier, A. P. (1989, June). *Report to the Alaska Area Native Health Service* (pp. 1–56).

Munhall, P. L. (Ed.). (1994). *In women's experience.* New York: NLN Press.

Murcia, A., & Stewart, B. (1989). *Helping the woman you love recover from breast cancer.* New York: St. Martin's Press.

National Alliance of Breast Cancer Organizations. (1995). *Presentation: Native American women and breast cancer.* Salish-Kootenai College, Tribal Health, Flathead Reservation, Pablo, MT: Author.

Newman, P. (1991). *Just in time: Notes from my wife.* New York: Limelight Editions.

Newman, P. (1994, May). Fighting back. *Life,* 85.

Nightingale, F. (1969). *Notes on nursing. What it is. What it is not.* New York: Dover. (Original work published 1860)

Noddings, N. (1984). *Caring: A feminist approach to ethics and moral education.* Berkeley: University of California Press.

Northouse, L. L. (1981, June). Mastectomy patients and the fear of cancer recurrance. *Cancer Nursing, 4*(3), 213–220.

Northouse, L. L. (1988). Social support in patient's and husband's adjustment to breast cancer. *Nursing Research, 37,* 91–95.

Nutting, P. A. et al. (1994). The danger of applying uniform clinical policies across populations: The case of breast cancer in American Indians. *American Journal of Public Health, 84,* 10.

Patkotak, P. (1994, June). Sure the bush is changing, but let it change slowly. *The Anchorage Daily News,* p. 10.

Peck, M. S. (1987). *The different drum: Community making and peace.* New York: Simon & Shuster.

Bibliography

Penn, J. (1991). Principles of tumor immunity: Immuncompetence and cancer. In V. DeVita, S. Hellman, & S. Rosenberger (Eds.), *Biologic therapy of cancer*. Philadelphia: Lippincott.

Perrone, B., Henrietta, H., & Krueger, V. (1989). *Medicine women, curanderas, and women doctors*. Norman: University of Oklahoma Press.

Presentation to the First Lady. (1993). From *Pathways to nursing education* (Pablo, MT: Salish Kootenai College, Flathead Reservation) Presented at Indian Health Care Reform, Washington, DC, March 15–16, 1993.

Raloff, J. (1994, January). The gender benders. *Science News, 145*, 24–27.

_____. (1994, April). Studies spark new tamoxifen controversy. *Science News, 145*, 133.

_____. (1994, April). FDA, others offer new tamoxifen warnings. *Science News, 145*, 247.

Renni, J. (1994, September). Malignant mimicry. *Scientific American, 269*, 34.

Ridington, R. (1988). *Train to heaven: Knowledge and narrative in a northern native community*. Iowa City: University of Iowa.

Rollins, B. (1976). *First you cry*. New York: Lippincott.

Rosenbaum, E. H., M.D. (1983). *Can you prevent cancer?* St. Louis: Mosby.

Ross, C. A. (1992, July/August). Vitamin A and protective immunity. *Nutrition Today, 27*, 18–26.

Rutquist, L. E. (1993, October 20). Mammogram as a source of breast cancer. *Journal of the National Cancer Institute*. Stockholm, Sweden: Karolinska Hospital.

Samuels, M., & Bennett, H. Z. (1983). *Well body, well earth*. San Francisco: Sierra Club Books.

Seltzer, V. L. (1991). *Every woman's guide to breast cancer: Prevention, treatment, recovery*. New York: Viking Press.

Schover, L. R. (1991, March, April). The impact of breast on sexuality, body image, and intimate relationships. *CA-Cancer Journal for Clinicians, 41*(2), 112–120.

Shapiro, S., Strax, P., & Venet, L. (1990, March, April). Evaluation of periodic breast cancer screening with mammography: Methodology and early observations. *CA-Cancer Journal for Clinicians, 40*(2), 111–125.

Shiva, V. (1993). *Staying alive*. Trowbridge, England: Dostesios.

Simone, C. B. (1992). *Cancer and nutrition*. Garden City, NY: Avery.

Smith, C. M., & Maurer, F. C. (1994). *Community health nursing*. Philadelphia: W.B. Saunders.

Spletter, M. (1982). *A woman's choice: New options in the treatment of breast cancer*. Boston: Beacon Press.

Stetz, K. (1990). A longitudinal study of the adjustment of patients and husbands to breast cancer. *Oncology Nursing Forum, 17*, 43–46.

Summary of the American Cancer Society Report to the nation: Cancer in the poor. (1990, September, October). *CA-Cancer Journal for Clinicians, 39*(5), 263–265.

Bibliography

The politics of cancer. (1993, November, December). *Utne Reader, 30,* 16–18.

United States Public Health and Human Services. (1993). *Healthy people 2000.* Boston: Jones and Bartlett.

Wall, S. (1994). *Wisdom's daughters.* New York: Harper Perennial.

Wallis, V. (1993). *Two old women.* New York: HarperCollins.

Waslien, C. I., & Rehwoldt, R. E. (1990, July, August). Micronutrients and antioxidents in processed foods—analysis of data from 1987 food additives survey. *Nutrition Today, 25,* 36–40.

Westkott, M. (1979). Feminist criticism of the social sciences. *The Harvard Review, 48*(4), 422–430.

Weinhouse, S. et al. (1991, November, December). American Cancer Society guidelines on diet, nutrition, and cancer. *CA-Cancer Journal for Clinicians, 41*(6), 334–338.

Weiss, R. (1992, September). Breast cancer, a complete guide to prevention plus an update on mammography. *American Health.*

Young, T. K. (1994). *The health of Native Americans.* New York: Oxford University Press.

Appendix A

Bergman, A., & Olsson, M. (1985). Pathology of the Baltic gray seal and ringed seal females with special references to adrenocortical hyperplasia: Is environmental pollution the cause of a widely distributed disease syndrome? *Finnish Game Research, 44,* 47–62.

Canoe, L. (1982). In B. Hungry Wolf (Ed.), *The ways of my grandmothers.* New York: Quill.

Coburn, T., Davidson, S., Green, R., Hodge, C., Jackson, C., & Linoff, R. (1990). *Great Lakes: Great legacy?* Washington, DC: The Conservation Foundation and The Institute for Research and Public Policy.

Davies, D., & Mes, J. (1987). Comparison of residue levels of some organochlorine compounds in breast milk of the general and indigenous Canadian population. *Bulletin of Environmental Contamination and Toxicology, 39,* 743–749.

Draper, H. H. (1977). The aboriginal Eskimo diet. *American Anthropologist, 79,* 309–316.

El-Bayoumy, K. (1992). Environmental carcinogens that may be involved in human breast cancer etiology. *Chemical Research in Toxicology, 5*(5), 585–590.

Falck, F., Ricci, M., Wolff, M. S. et al. (1992). Pesticides and polychlorinated biphenyl residues in human breast lipids and their relation to breast cancer. *Archives of Environmental Health, 47,* 143–146.

Fox, G. (1992). Epidemiological and pathobiological evidence of contaminant-induced alterations in sexual development in free living wildlife. In *The wildlife human connection.* Princeton, NJ: Princeton Scientific.

Grubbs, C. (1992). Research on caritonoids goes beyond beta carotene. *American Institute for Cancer Research.*

Bibliography

Jacobson, J., Jacobson, S., & Humphry, H. (1990). Effects of in utero exposure to poly-chlorinated biphenyls and related contaminants on cognitive functioning in young children. *Journal of Pediatrics, 116,* 38–45.

Lazneby, R. (1993, June, July). Chlorine. *Earthkeeper: Canada's Environmental Magazine, 5,* 111.

Lowell, J. (1990). PCBs in Inuit women's breast milk. In M. Crnkovich (Ed.), *"Gossip": A spoken history of women in the North.* Ottawa, Ontario: Canadian Arctic Resources Committee.

Perera, F. P. (1990, September, October). Molecular epidemiology: A new tool in assessing risks of environmental carcinogens. *CA-Cancer Journal for Clinicians, 40*(5), 277–288.

Raloff, J. (1994, January). Something's fishy. *Science News, 146,* 8–9.

Ramsey, M. (1993). *Metabolism in polar bears.* Lecture delivered at the Northern Studies Centre, Churchill, Manitoba.

Ruben, B. (1993). Protecting Mother Earth's bottom line. *Environmental Action.* Takoma Park, MD.

Sugimura, S. (1986). Studies on environmental chemical carcinogenesis in Japan. *Science, 223,* 312–317.

Swain, W. (1991). Effects of organochlorine chemicals on the reproductive outcome of humans who consumed contaminated Great Lakes fish: An epidemiologic consideration. *Journal of Toxicology and Environmental Health, 33,* 587–639.

Taubes, G. (1994). Pesticides and breast cancer, no link? *Science, 226,* 88–89.

Tilson, H., Jacobson, J., & Rogan, W. (1990). Polychlorinated biphenyl and the developing nervous system: Cross species comparisons. *Neurotoxicology and Tetrogology, 12,* 239–248.

Travis, J. (1994, December 23). Taking a bottom-to-sky "slice" of the Arctic Ocean. *Science, 226,* 23.

Thornton, J. (1993). *Chlorine, human health and the environment: The breast cancer warning.* Washington, DC: Greenpeace.

Thornton, J. (1991). *Chlorine: The product is poison: The case for a chlorine phase out.* Chicago: Greenpeace.

Twitchell, K. (1990, February, March). The not so pristine Arctic: From plankton to polar bears, the food chain is contaminated by global pollution. *Canadian Geographic,* 53–55.

Unger, M., Kaiser, H., Bilchert-Toft, M., Olsen, J., & Clausen, J. (1984). Organochlorine compounds in human breast fat from diseased and without breast cancer and in a biopsy material from newly diagnosed patients undergoing breast surgery. *Environmental Research, 34,* 24–28.

Usme, S., & Toledo, M. (1993). WEDO hearing examines the environmental links to breast cancer. *WEDO-Women's Environment and Development Organization.* New York: Women USA Fund.

Bibliography

Wolff, M., Tolino, P., Lee, E., Rivera, N., & Dubin, N. (1993). Blood levels of organochlorine residues and risk of breast cancer. *Journal of National Cancer Institute*, *85*(8), 648–652.

Wolff, M. (1993, February). Comments on the Greenpeace report "Breast cancer and the environment: The chlorine connection" and on the Chlorine Institute's response. Washington, DC: Greenpeace.

For further reading concerning carcinogenic organochlorines, please refer to: International Agency for Research on Cancer, World Health Organization, Lyons, France. Data from National Library of Medicine, Registry of the Toxic Effects of Chemical Substances, Bethesda, Maryland.

Appendix B

Brady, J. (1990). *One in three women confront the cancer epidemic.* Chicago: Third Side Press.

Burhansstipanov, L. (1993). *Documentation of the cancer research needs of American Indians and Alaska natives.* Washington, DC: National Institute of Health, National Cancer Institute, United States Department of Health and Human Services.

Codel, R. B. (1985, November). Potential contamination of surface water supplies by atmospheric releases from nuclear plants. *Health Physics, 49,* 713–730.

Eskin, B. A., Focog, J. A. P., Bassett, J. G., & George, D. L. (1974, September). Human breast uptake of radioactive iodine. *Obstetrics and Gynecology, 44,* 398.

Fackelman, K. (1993, October). Weighing risks, benefits of mammography. *Science News, 144*(23), 262.

Halford, D. K., & Markham, O. D. (1984, June). Iodine-129 in waterfowl muscle from a radioactive leaching pond complex in southeastern Idaho. *Health Physics, 46,* 1259–1263.

Hansen, W. C. (1993, May 2–7). Radioactive contamination in Arctic Tundra ecosystems. Arctic research of the United States. *Proceedings of the Interagency Arctic Research Policy Committee, Workshop on Arctic Contamination, 8,* 198–206.

Hopkins, B. J. (1967, February). The retention of Strontium-90 transferred through milk (and placenta) in rat offspring. *Health Physics, 13,* 973–976.

Kalinnikov, V. T. (1993, May). *Mining and metallurgic waste as a source of Arctic contamination and a remedy for northern environmental protection.* Paper presented at the Workshop on Arctic Contamination, Anchorage, AK.

Koch, J., & Tadmor, J. (1986, June). Radfood-A dynamic model for radioactivity transfer through the human food chain. *Health Physics, 50,* 721–737.

Mahara, Y., & Kudo, A. (1981, October). Fixation and mobilization of CO-60 on sediments in coastal environments. *Health Physics, 41,* 645–655.

_____. (1981). Interaction and mobility of CO-60 between water and sediments in marine environments: Possible effects by acid rain. *Water Research, 15,* 413–419.

Bibliography

Mahon, D. C., & Matthewes, R. W. (1983). Seasonal variation in the accumulation of radionuclides of the uranium series by Yellow Pond Lily (Nuphar lutea). *Bulletin of Environmental Toxicology, 30,* 575–581.

Makeyev, V. V. (1993, May). *Research into bottom sedimentation in the Arctic.* Paper presented at the Workshop on Arctic Contamination, Anchorage, AK.

Maksimovsky, V. A. (1993, May). *Sources of technogic radionuclide pollution (STRP) in the southern Arctic ocean.* Paper presented at the Workshop on Arctic Contamination, Anchorage, AK.

Markham, O. D., Hakonson, T. E., Whicker, F. W., & Morton, J. S. (1983, July). Iodine-129 in Mule Deer thyroids in the Rocky Mountain west. *Health Physics, 45,* 31–37.

Matishov, G. M. (1993, May). *Radionuclides in ecosystems of Barents and Karsky Seas, Arctic archipelagos and coastlines.* Paper presented at the Workshop on Arctic Contamination, Anchorage, AK.

McCloud, K. W., Alberts, J. J., Adriano, D. K., & Pinder, J. E. III (1984, February). Plutonium contents of broadleaf vegetable crops grown near a nuclear fuel chemical separations facility. *Health Physics, 46,* 261–267.

Swanson, S. M. (1985, November). Food transfer of U-Series radionuclides in northern Saskatchewan aquatic system. *Health Physics, 49,* 747–770.

Tokunaga, M. (1978, August). Breast cancer among atomic bomb survivors. In *Acta pathology Japan* (pp. 197–209). Kagoshima, Japan: Kagoshima University, School of Medicine, The Second Department of Pathology.

Watabe, T., & Kamada, H. (1984, June). Airborne radionuclides onto pine needles collected in the vicinity of the nuclear power plant. *Journal of Radiation Research, 25,* 140–149.

Appendix C

Agresti, A., & Finlay B. (1984). *Statistical methods for the social sciences.* San Francisco: Dillen.

Altmann, J. (1974). Observational study of behavior: Sampling methods. *Behavior, 49,* 227–267.

Achterberg, J. (1991). *Woman as healer.* Boston: Shambala Press.

Atkinson, P., & Hammersley, M. (1983). *Ethnography: Principles in practice.* London: Tavistock.

Babbie, E. (1992). *The practice of social research.* Belmont, CA: Wadsworth.

Becker, H. S., & Geer, B. (1957). Participant observation and interviewing: A comparison? *Human organization, 23,* 28–32.

Bleier, R. (Ed.). (1984). *Science and gender: A critique of biology and its theories on women.* New York: Pergamon Press.

Bleier, R. (Ed.). (1986). *Feminist approaches to science.* New York: Pergamon Press.

Bibliography

Burhansstipanov, L. (1993). *Documentation of the cancer research needs of American Indians and Alaska Natives.* Washington, DC: National Institutes of Health, National Cancer Institute, U.S. Department of Health and Human Services.

Bowles, G., & Duelli-Klein, R. (Eds.). (1983). *Theories of womens' studies.* Boston: Routledge & Kegan Paul.

Brady, J. (1990). *One in three women confront the cancer epidemic.* Chicago: Third Side Press.

_____. (1989). *Cancer as a woman's issue.* Chicago: Third Side Press.

Campbell-Hurd, K. (1938). *A history of women in medicine.* Haddam, CT: Haddam Press.

Coles, R., & Coles, J. H. (1978). *Women of crisis.* New York: Delta.

Culley, M., & Pourteges, C. (1985). *Gendered subjects: The dynamics of feminist teaching.* Boston: Routledge & Kegan Paul.

Denzin, N. K. (Ed.). (1970). *Sociological methods: A source book.* London: Butterworth.

Donovan, J. (1992). *Feminist theory.* New York: Continuum.

Drew, R. P., & Hardman, M. L. (1985). *Designing and conducting behavioral research* (4th ed.). New York: MacMillan.

Duelli-Klein, R., & Bowles, G. (Eds.). (1983). *Theories of women's studies.* London: Routledge & Kegan Paul.

Eisley, R. (1988). *The chalice and the blade.* San Francisco: HarperCollins.

Ellman, M. (1968). *Thinking about women.* London: Macmillan. Bloomington: Indiana University Press.

Fee, E. (1981). Is feminism a threat to scientific objectivity? *International Journal of Women's Studies, 4,* 378–392.

Fonow, M., & Cook, J. (Eds.). (1991). *Beyond methodology, feminist scholarship as lived research.* Bloomington: Indiana University Press.

Fransella, F., & Frost, K. (1977). *On being a woman.* London: Tavistock.

Galtung, J. (1967). *Theory and methods of social research.* London: Allen & Unwin.

Getting along in Labrador. (1975). Calgary: Petro-Canada.

Gluck, S., & Patei, D. S. (Eds.). (1991). *Women's words: The feminist practice of oral history.* New York: Routledge.

Gilligan, C. (1982). *In a different voice.* Cambridge, MA: Harvard University Press.

Grant, L., Ward, K., & Rong, X. L. (1987). Is there an association between gender and method in sociological research? *American Sociological Review, 52,* 586–562.

Harding, S., & Hintikka, M. (Eds.). (1983). *Discovering reality: Feminist perspectives on epistemology, metaphysics, methodology, and philosophy of science.* Boston: Reidel.

Hood, J. C., & Fox, M. L. (Eds.). (1985). The lone scholar myth. In *Scholarly writing and publishing: Issues, problems, and solutions* pp. 111–121. Boulder, CO: Westview Press.

Hochschild, A. R. (1975). *Another voice: Feminists perspectives on social life and social science.* New York: Anchor Books.

Hooks, B. (1984). *Feminist theory from margin to center.* Chicago: South End Press.

Bibliography

Hubbard, R. (1990). *The politics of womens' biology.* New Brunswick, NJ: Rutgers University Press.

Ives, E. D. (1980). *The tape recorded interview.* Knoxville, TN: University of Tennessee Press.

Jayaratine, T. E. (1983). The value of quantitative methodology for feminist research. In G. Bowles & R. Duelli-Klein (Eds.), *Theories of women's studies,* pp. 140–161. Boston: Routledge.

Keller, E. F. (1985). *Reflections on gender and science.* New Haven, CT: Yale University Press.

Kelly, A. (1978). Feminism and research. *Women's Studies International Quarterly, 1,* 225–232.

Langland, E., & Grove, W. (Eds.). (1981). *A feminist perspective in the academy.* Chicago: University of Chicago Press. Research Conference, Loughborough, England.

Lanier, A. (1993, October, November, December). Epidemiology of cancer in Alaska Natives. *Alaska Medicine, 32,* 240–272.

Locke, L. F., Spirduso, W. W., & Silverman, S. J. (1987). *Proposals that work.* Newbury Park, CA: Sage.

Meleis, A. I., Arruda, E. N., Lane, S., & Bermal, P. (1994). Veiled, voluminous, and devalued: Narrative stories about low income women from Brazil, Egypt, and Columbia. *Advanced Nursing Science, 17*(2), 1–15.

Moustakas, C. (1990). *Heuristic research.* Newbury Park, CA: Sage.

Patten, M. (1989). *Qualitative research.* Newbury Park, CA: Sage.

Powdermaker, H. (1966). *Stranger and friend: The way of the anthropologist.* New York: W.W. Norton.

Reinharz, S. (1979). *On becoming a social scientist.* San Francisco: Jossey Press.

Reinharz, S. (1991). *Feminist methods in social research.* New York: Pergamon Books.

Roberts, H. (1981). *Doing feminist research.* Boston: Routledge & Kegan Paul.

Rosser, S. (1988). *Feminism within the science and health care professions: Overcoming resistance.* Oxford: Pergamon Press.

Ruth, S. (1980). *Issues in feminism: A first course in womens' studies.* Boston: Houghton Mifflin.

Signell, K. A. (1990). *Wisdom of the heart.* New York: Bantam Books.

Stanley, L. (1979). Feminist research, feminist consciousness and experiences of sexism. *Women's Studies International Quarterly, 2,* 359–379.

Stocker, M. (1991). *Cancer as a women's issue.* Chicago: Third Side Press.

Williams, F. (1992). *Reasoning with statistics.* New York: Harcourt Brace Jovanovich.

Zweig, F. (1949). *Labour, life and poverty.* London: Gollancz.

Zola, I. K. (1983). *Sociomedical enquiries.* Philadelphia: Temple University Press.

Index

Index